An

HEALED
OVERNIGHT

Five Steps to Accessing
Supernatural Healing

Healed Overnight! *Five Steps to Accessing Your Supernatural Healing*
©Copyright 2016 by Amy Keesee Freudiger.
All rights reserved.
ISBN 978-1-945177-39-2

Unless otherwise noted, all scriptures quoted are from the New International Version (NIV) of the Holy Bible®, NIV®. Copyright © 1973, 1978, 1984, 2011 by Biblica, Inc.® Used by permission. All rights reserved worldwide.

Scriptures marked (NLT) are from the Holy Bible, New Living Translation® Copyright© 1996, 2004, 2007, 2013 by Tyndale House Foundation. Used by permission of Tyndale House Publishers, Inc., Carol Stream, Illinois 60188. All rights reserved. New Living, NLT, and the New Living Translation logo are registered trademarks of Tyndale House Publishers.

Scriptures marked (MSG) are from The Message. Copyright© 1993, 1994, 1995, 1996, 2000, 2001, 2002. Used by permission of NavPress Publishing Group.

Scriptures marked (NASB) are from the New American Standard Bible, Copyright © 1960,1962,1963,1968, 1971,1972,1973,1975,1977,1995 by The Lockman Foundation. Used by permission.

Scriptures marked (KJV) are from the King James Version of the Holy Bible.

Published by Honest Beauty Publishing
Printed in the United States of America.

Author's Note: I do not capitalize the name "satan" because I do not ascribe him even that small honor.

Cover photography: Ryan Jacquot Photography
Graphic Design: Ryan Dame

*Dedicated to my husband, Jason,
who loved me back to life.*

*And to my parents, Gary and Drenda
Keesee, who taught me how to believe
God for the impossible.*

TABLE OF CONTENTS

FOREWORD

Amy's healing story is one of the most incredible we have witnessed in our ministry years, and is so very personal to us since she is our precious daughter. As her mother, I witnessed Amy's struggle to work through the spiritual and emotional battles, not to mention the physical pain of illness. After searching for answers from doctor after doctor and even the Internet to no avail, I watched as Amy made a decision and "all in" commitment to possess God's promises for her life and health. The morning she awoke completely healed and called me in tears of joy is unforgettable.

Our God is a healer and you can have His promises come to pass no matter what circumstance you face—just follow Amy's journey and do what she did by faith. I have witnessed her minister healing to many others with compassion and great power over sickness. Amy is an anointed worship leader (the purest worshipper of God I know), and one of His most tender, thoughtful people. When she faced physical pain and emotionally challenging disfigurement, we all struggled to understand how this could happen to her. Discovering the real origin of sickness and the answer God provides to combat it changed everything! Without any medical interventions, today she is healed and completely whole, fulfilling her destiny in Christ.

—Drenda Keesee
Author, Speaker, Pastor, and Television Host

INTRODUCTION

All teenagers have a certain feeling of invincibility. I was no exception. But at age 18 I found myself in a downhill physical battle that lasted nine years.

A growth in my abdomen had grown to the size of 13 pounds, the equivalent weight of 15 cans of soda or a large bowling ball. I looked six months pregnant. My spine had so much pressure on it that it was straight in the lower part and the vertebrae stuck out. My lower abdomen often ached, and I could not lay on my stomach. The muscles in my legs always hurt. I had digestion issues. Eating often made me feel nauseous. My organs were displaced by the growth.

I suffered several infections. People who didn't know me were constantly asking if I were pregnant. I struggled with symptoms for so long, they became the lens through which I viewed myself. I hated my body because of it.

But the morning I woke up totally and completely healed, all that changed! I lost 13 pounds and 9 inches in my waist. Gone.

I remember the morning I woke up healed just like it were yesterday. The shock. The relief. The almost numb feeling of not being in any pain or discomfort. I sat up in bed and knew something felt strange. But my husband was the one who looked at me and said, "Go look in the mirror."

All the pain was over. All the heartache ceased in an instant. My body was healed overnight in a divine encounter with the supernatural realm. The healing was made possible, however, by months of lessons learned that I want to share with you.

In this book you will learn:

    —Five supernatural steps to receiving your miracle

    —Practical examples of how to apply these principles to your life

    —Other people's real stories of supernatural healing

    —Healing scriptures and confessions for meditation

    —Answers to big questions concerning miracles and healing

There were many lessons I learned through my journey that I can't wait to share with you in this book, woven into the incredible story of how I was healed overnight. I wanted this book to be small enough that you can keep it in your briefcase, purse, or car and pull it out again and again. I also encourage you to keep extra copies to hand out to others who may be facing illness.

The thing is, anyone can be healed using the supernatural principles I learned. That's right, I said everyone, and that includes you. I don't know your situation, and I don't know what doctors, family members, friends, or co-workers have told you. I don't know the name of your diagnosis, but I know a Name that trumps every other name. And I do know that for every problem you face in your life, there is an Answer. There is hope.

Let me share my experience, my failures, my lessons, and my perspective on how I was healed overnight. I am also excited to tell you other real life stories from others who experienced miraculous healings confirmed by doctors.

Miracles are real. The supernatural world is real. Scientific studies are confirming this! So I invite you into my story—and into the supernatural realm where nothing is impossible.

My story could be your story. Get ready for an encounter with miracles.

CHAPTER ONE

MY TRUE STORY

"Now faith is the substance of things hoped for, the evidence of things not seen."

Hebrews 11:1 (KJV)

Some things are too amazing to be mere coincidence. Some things are so far beyond scientific human understanding that we must ask questions. We must dive in deeper, beyond the perfunctory, "Well, it was a coincidence," or, "Fate was kind to you." That's the case with my story. It still blows me away, even though I was the one who experienced it.

In 2001, I was a very healthy and active 18-year-old with plenty of dreams. I was working on an Associates degree in Fine Arts and was ready to take on all that life would bring. From choir and musical courses, to art classes and graphic design courses, I immersed myself in the creative side of life. I was a hard worker, earning straight A's through school, and I thought nothing could slow me down.

One slight annoyance. I seemed to be gaining weight in my torso, so I started watching what I ate. Instead of the typical "freshman 15" pounds gained, I lost 15 pounds that year.

Two years later, on a warm, sunny May day, I got ready for the final rehearsal of my senior vocal recital with my accompanist and vocal coach. Only a few more days and I would be standing in front of a recital hall full of people, trying to calm my jitters and remember all the lyrics to the arias and art songs I would be singing in English, Italian, German, and Latin. Today's rehearsal was important, indeed. Plus, a photographer was dropping in to take pictures for a story in the school newspaper.

Better fix my hair, I thought, as I slipped into a colorful top and tugged at my curly brown hair. I took a deep breath to steady my mind. I was feeling overwhelmed, with final papers and tests due, the school musical coming up, and now my senior recital. I also actively served in my church and worked part-time for my dad's company. "I can do this," I told myself.

After singing through my music at the rehearsal, my teacher took my hand and encouraged me. "This is it! You're going to do so well. Relax!" Then the photographer stepped up and said, "Smile!" Like all we women do while getting a picture taken, I stood up tall and sucked in my tummy...only it wouldn't go in. I noticed it and thought, *That's strange.* It felt like those muscles were not working, or something was in their way.

When something seems wrong with our bodies, most of us try to dismiss it. We will tell ourselves, *Oh, it's probably no big deal. It'll go away.* We push it to the back of our minds and go on with life. I certainly did not have time to think about this problem right now. But it kept bothering me.

That week I stood in front of the mirror and felt my stomach, trying to suck it in. It didn't move. It felt hard. I just figured I was bloated or not drinking enough water. Too much stress. Something like that.

That Friday night, I performed my senior recital in front of a full music hall. My teacher had prepared me well, and I did it! I didn't forget a word and was able to maintain the energy and vocal stamina required for a full operatic concert. There would be more papers to write and more finals to take in the coming days before I would officially graduate with my Associates and go on to get my Bachelor's degree. But in that moment, I forgot all that and soaked in the accomplishment.

Collapsing in bed that night with a contented sigh, I rolled onto my belly and noticed that my back started to hurt. A dull ache started in my abdomen. I rolled onto my back and chalked it up to all the standing I had done that night.

Over the next few months, my belly started to feel weird. I could push on it and it literally would not budge. Worry started to nag at my mind. The muscles in my abdomen got harder. I finally stopped dismissing the problem when my stomach started actually protruding.

I was now 20 years old, a season when

self-consciousness takes on a whole new meaning because everyone starts asking you about finding "the one" and getting married. Beyond the typical self-consciousness, I became extremely sensitive about my body and my looks. I felt so utterly ugly when my stomach started sticking out.

Maybe I just gain weight in a weird way, I told myself. So I started working out and being even more careful about what I ate. I was a tall girl at 5'9, and my once proportionate body now looked awkward. My arms and legs got thinner, but my stomach only got bigger. My clothes stopped fitting. Something was wrong.

I'm a very private person, and because I thought the cause was simple weight gain, I didn't bring it up to my mom at all for a long time. She finally asked me if I was okay one day when she hugged me and felt my tummy sticking out. I told her that I could no longer lay on my stomach in bed without it aching, and that I had lost the ability to pull my stomach in. She asked me a few more questions just as the doorbell rang. It was our personal trainer, who came for a weekly workout session with my brothers and me. "I'm sure it's fine," I told my mom, trying to ease the worry on her face. "Hey, there's the doorbell! It seems so strange to say we have a 'personal trainer,'" I laughed, trying to change the subject. After all, when I was young, my family didn't have two nickels to rub together. But my dad's business had flourished and things had gotten better financially for us.

My mom smiled and said, "Well, we've got to stay healthy if we're going to travel the world." My mom and I both share a love of travel, and we often dreamed about where we wanted to go. Now I worried that something serious could stop all those dreams.

As we ended the day's workout, my mom brought up my symptoms to our trainer. He did some stretches and abdominal exercises with me while observing my muscles. "They aren't moving or responding to anything," he said, puzzled. "It could be a muscle imbalance, but I'd see a doctor about it," he concluded.

My mom took me to an endocrinologist a few weeks later. I was extremely nervous, and I envisioned the doctor telling me I had some terminal illness. Fear started messing with my mind. As I sat on the exam table and the doctor came in, I could tell she was in a hurry. She asked me a few questions as she quickly felt my stomach and back. I explained that I couldn't lose weight in my stomach area, and I couldn't pull it in.

Having never known me prior to this, it was impossible for her to feel or see the change in my body. My shape *had* changed over the past few months, but she had no reference point. She simply said, "Go to this doctor and have your hormones checked to rule out PCOS or Crohn's, but you don't have any other symptoms associated with those illnesses. ***It's probably just the way you are.*** " Those words smacked me between the eyes. She continued somewhat condescendingly, "We all have our problem areas, our flaws, things we don't like about our bodies."

Well, I didn't want to hear I had a terminal illness, but I also didn't want to hear that I was terminally flawed, either! I felt like all the oxygen had been sucked out of the room, and all my hope with it. I wanted to say, "That's it? This is the way I am? You can't help me? I'm stuck like this forever?" but I kept quiet. My mom asked about an ultrasound or scan. She didn't think that was necessary at this point. She made it known she was out of time and hurried out of the room. *Well, now what? Am I crazy or is there really something wrong with me?*

Despite the brush-off from this doctor, Mom and I *knew* something had changed in my body. A few weeks later, we were off to a hormone therapist. We explained the issues to him, and he did some blood work. On our second visit, he gave me the results and said that everything looked pretty good. No markers for Crohn's or PCOS. His opinion was, "The problems in your body might be due to your spinal structure or a muscular imbalance. You'll probably ***just have to live with it.***" This was the second time I'd been told that. A little voice kept whispering in my head, *"This is just the way I am shaped. Deal with it. It may get worse. Who knows? You'll always be ugly like this."*

Both doctors had seemed unconcerned, so I began thinking that perhaps I was just imagining things. Or maybe I was just fat. My mom suggested the potential for an ovarian cyst, but they suggested we wait and see if it got worse.

My abdomen was now protruding to the point that on several occasions people asked if I was pregnant. The first time I got the question, "When are you due?" I was crushed. I cried myself to sleep that night. And every night after I got that question, because it happened often. As scary as the physical symptoms were, the emotional embarrassment of these questions and of my appearance were worse. Devastating, even. Being in the formative stage of early adulthood, it was a serious blow to my body image.

My back started to feel stiff all the time. When I worked out or jogged, the muscles in my abs, legs, and back would become so tight, it was difficult to stretch. Things like pulling my foot up behind me to stretch my quadriceps became impossible. I stopped my jogging routine altogether because of the pain.

I weighed about 135 pounds at over 5'9" tall, so I wasn't "fat," but I felt huge due to my shape. I condemned myself anytime I ate something "unhealthy" because I didn't want to get "fatter." Shame about my body followed me into every dressing room whenever I would try on clothes. I limited my wardrobe to maternity-like shirts and dresses. I did everything I could to disguise the issue. I would wear loose-fitting shirts and lots of scarves and jackets to hide my stomach.

I hated how I looked!

I began to accept the fact that my body was defective. That I would be like this forever. That I would never like myself nor be able to wear normal clothing. That I would have to continue to limit my physical activities. That strangers would continue to ask if I was pregnant. Maybe I would never be married because maybe no one would ever think I was attractive.

The despair and self-hatred grew stronger, and my hope grew weaker. I would dream of being able to wear a swimsuit without feeling embarrassed. I would imagine being able to walk in high-heeled shoes without dealing with debilitating aches for days afterward. I started to hate every part of me. I thought, *If only I was normal. If only I looked like so-and-so. If only my boobs were bigger and my stomach smaller and my nose straighter and my ears cuter and....*

On and on the self-criticism would go, like a bad movie I could never shut off.

Despite my parents' encouragement and love, I secretly hated *me*.

LETTING GO OF DREAMS

I had several dreams for my life: travel on missions, record music, and create art. In my early twenties I had some opportunities to pursue some of those dreams.

Soon after graduating college, the music director at our small church took a job in another state and felt I was the one to take over his position. I had been singing on the team for several years, but I felt very inadequate to take this position. "I think you have the wrong person," I laughed. Still, music was part of what I wanted to do with my life, and everyone was very supportive, so I accepted. From college right into leading a volunteer music team of 20 people, I just started getting used to living out of my comfort zone.

One night after a Wednesday night service, a newcomer to the church came up to compliment the music and then asked, "So are you pregnant?" "Uh, no. No, I'm not. Just need to cut back a little I guess," I tried to joke. The knife in my heart wouldn't let me smile. My mind started telling me, *You shouldn't be on that stage leading music. Look at you. You're an embarrassment.* I seriously wanted to quit so many times.

The chance to fulfill my dream of traveling on missions trips came up when our youth group planned a trip to Albania, the poorest country in Eastern Europe. It was such an incredible experience to be able to help out in orphanages and churches around the country and in the capital city of Tirana! I fell in love with the people. But on our last day there, I had three different people ask about my baby and when I was due. And it happened in front of my friends, no less! I was so incredibly embarrassed, I wanted to hide.

Even though I loved missions, again my mind told me I couldn't do it. It was just too embarrassing and emotionally draining. How could I teach others about love when I couldn't love myself?

ON THE ALBANIA-ITALY MISSIONS TRIP

On the outside, I tried not to let the inner struggles and pain slow me down, mostly because I didn't want anyone to think something was wrong with me. My thoughts started to be consumed with keeping a certain front up when I was around others.

I had been writing songs since childhood, and people always commented that I should record an album. I could get lost in making music, and the songs just kept coming to me. I saved the money, found a producer, and recorded my first solo album in 2005.

The day I wrapped up my final mixing session, I also went into a photo shoot for the album cover. During the shoot, the photographer kept encouraging me, "Just pull your tummy in," or, "Skinny pose." Only I couldn't. I wanted to burst into tears and run out of the studio. I just knew I would hate every photo.

When my album released, my band and I started doing some concerts around my home state. I remember well the last concert I did. It was my last concert because at the end of it, a woman came up and said, "So, you're pregnant, right?" Her tone had an accusatory sound. After all, during the concert I had shared about being single and saving my virginity for when I was married. "No, I'm not," I whimpered. "What?! You have to be! Are you sure?" she said loudly. "Yes ma'am, I'm very sure, thank you," I huffed.

I never wanted to do a concert ever again.

Disappointments started swallowing my dreams, till I just kind of gave up on them.

The trenches of self-hatred were dug even deeper every time someone made a comment about my body, and I never got used to it. One family spread rumors about me, accusing me of sleeping around and getting pregnant. On the surface, I would try to dismiss it. But on the inside, I was devastated.

I went through a whole season of disappointments, setbacks, failures, and hurts. I stifled it all under a smile and kept myself very busy. However, the embarrassment over my body would inevitably resurface. I stopped pursuing my dreams passionately. I started backing down. I didn't want to face people.

GROWING UP YEARS

Let me pause here and share more about my background. I grew up in a family that believes in out-of-the-ordinary things—supernatural things. My parents raised my four siblings and me in church and taught us that God is real. They also taught us that nothing is impossible if we will just believe. That doesn't mean I never questioned my faith at times in my life, but deep down I always knew the truth. My parents created an environment in our home that allowed us to discover and explore faith.

I guess there's never really been a time when I didn't believe in God. Maybe you don't believe in Him, but I dare you to keep reading. I challenge you to open your mind to what I'm going to tell you.

From a very young age, I had encounters with the power of God. At times, His power and love would overwhelm me until I couldn't stand. Sometimes, I would see visions of things to come, and they would happen. A few times, I prayed for sick people and they were healed. Most of all, I wanted everyone to know about God.

I remember being seven years old and just weeping my heart out to think that there were people who didn't know God. I wanted to tell everyone that miracles were real, and that God loved them. I was extremely sensitive to people's hurts and pains as a young girl. I wanted to alleviate suffering. I told my parents I would be a missionary when I grew up.

One supernatural occurrence was especially vivid. When I was eight years old, my family was in a severe car accident, in which a man pulled out in front of us, and we hit him at 60 miles per hour. Astoundingly, we all walked away with minor cuts and bruises. That shouldn't have happened. My mom, six months pregnant, should have miscarried my sister after hitting the windshield and dash so hard, but she didn't. My little brother Tom didn't even have his seat belt on, but an angel must have held him inside that wrecked car, because he didn't get a scratch. I did end up with scars around my eye area from shattering glass.

When I was 15, the scars really started to make me mad. One night, I prayed a simple prayer and said, "God, I don't like these scars, and I'd appreciate it if you'd remove them. Thank you." The next week, I stepped in front of the bathroom mirror and noticed that the prominent scars had *completely* disappeared. That's impossible, but it happened.

Fast-forwarding to my twenties, I now had some deeper scars than what glass could leave. The anguish over my body and the shame of what people said about it felt too deep for God to simply erase.

I kept most of my feelings to myself. I didn't even let my family in on the hopelessness that waged a war in my heart. There's no way to really describe what it's like to hurt inside so deeply, yet feel like you can't tell anyone. Isolated and alone, I poured my heart into journal after journal, year after year. Maybe you know what I'm talking about because you've been in a dark place before. Maybe you're there right now. Hold on, things always get darkest before the dawn.

A GOD ENCOUNTER

Not only did I battle self-hatred, but also I fought fear. Worry, anxiousness, nervousness, and even anxiety attacks were a part of my life. I was very private about this side of me. Inside, my heart was divided.

Every day, fear would come knocking at my door, and I would let it in. Fear would do debilitating things to me. Fear would say things to me that messed up my life. I battled all sorts of fears. Fear of people. Fear of death. Fear of failure. Fear of being wrong. Fear of judgment. You name it. It was a constant abusive force in my life. It came disguised as "safety" oftentimes, but it was really control and bondage. Freedom seemed far away.

One humid night at a church youth camp, I was leading worship in an open air pavilion full of teenagers. Now you'd think that teenagers would want to get done with the service so they could go have fun. But the kids just kept praying and praying, lying on their faces to seek God. Our voices, lifted in song, grew louder and more fervent. Our hearts cried out as one for a revelation of God, Himself.

About two hours into the service, I encountered a powerful ray of light breaking into my heart. It was a presence more real than my problems, more powerful than my pain. "Jesus, is that you?" I whispered. I felt a surge of assurance and acceptance and security and worth and approval unlike I'd ever felt before. He loved me! I finally knew it!

That night, the God of the universe came and held His broken daughter close. And He didn't let go.

Love. I hadn't let myself feel loved for a long time. Oh sure, I knew people loved me. But I never let it soak into my emotions and my heart.

In a flash of memories, God showed me how satan had distorted my perception. A broken perception of myself resulted in me breaking the Law of Love, which is the most important commandment:

Jesus replied, "'Love the Lord

your God with all your heart
and with all your soul and with
all your mind.' This is the first
and greatest commandment. And
the second is like it: 'Love your
neighbor as yourself.' All the Law
and the Prophets hang on these two
commandments." (Matt. 22:38-40)

Do you see it? We can only love
our neighbor if we love God *and love
ourselves.* Plus, we can only love others
to the proportion we love ourselves.
The Law of Love requires us to consider
ourselves worthy of love. I learned that
if there is hatred toward ourselves, it's
impossible to receive healing.

***First, God had to restore love and
identity to my life.*** (I will share more on
this principle later.) First Corinthians 13:13
says, "And now these three remain: faith,
hope and love. But the greatest of these is
love." Without knowing you're loved,

you can't have hope for life, and without hope, you can't have faith to believe in anything. Love is the foundation upon which the walls of hope can rest. Faith is the roof that goes on top of the walls of hope. And the Holy Spirit can then come in and furnish that house (bring the needed miracle).

The Master Builder was doing some serious rebuilding on my foundation that night at youth camp. Tears mingled with sweat and ran down my face in the heat, as Love, Himself came near. I felt Him. It was like liquid acceptance poured over me, and I heart Him saying, "I'm proud of you. You're perfect. You're so lovely. There's nothing you can do to stop me from loving you. You please me so much."

First John 4:8 says, "Whoever does not love does not know God, because God is love." That night, I saw who He is—love. I realized that I had kept His acceptance at arm's length because I was filled with shame and unworthiness. Then, fear and insecurity (the natural results of a love deficit) had moved in, too.

That night, the darkness that had surrounded my life was shaken. Self-hatred had a lighter hold on me now, though it was not yet totally destroyed. Freedom started to dawn upon my heart, and the dark thoughts of the past started to blow away like reeds in the wind. Though it would take years to find total freedom and healing, the foundation was laid.

I remember one of my darkest moments that had happened a few weeks before that youth camp. I stood in front of the copper-framed mirror in my bathroom looking at my body, and I said through tears, "I hate myself. I hate you, body. You're so ugly. I can't stand you anymore!" Suddenly, I felt a stern rebuke from God, saying, "How can you say that about someone I love so much?" I drew my breath in, shocked. "I'm sorry, God," I mumbled, but I still didn't understand why He loved me.

I saw the ugliness of my thoughts—thoughts such as, *You are damaged goods. Who would want to love you? You are broken. You are ugly. You are not worthy of affection. You will always be alone. You will always be in pain because that's what you deserve. No one will ever love you.* (Maybe you have had thoughts like this at some time or another.)

So I started doing something new. I would stand in front of my mirror and say, "I love myself because I'm a daughter of God. I am precious, valuable, lovable, and beautiful. I love my body." Sometimes I would say these things through stinging tears of doubt. I was still learning how to believe those words.

Those voices of self-hatred have to shut up if we start speaking love. The voice of love silences the voice of hate. Light dispels darkness. It's no contest; love is always greater than hatred!

I realized that when I rejected myself, I

was rejecting God, because I was made in His image. Genesis 1:27 (NLT) says, "So God created human beings in his own image. In the image of God he created them; male and female he created them." If the evil one can get us to reject ourselves, we will ultimately reject God. If we reject ourselves, we also can never live in our destinies.

Self-hatred causes us to abort our dreams. It causes us to pass up on God's plan. It brings destruction to our futures and to our families. Satan wants to twist our self-images until we can no longer recognize

IN MY TWENTIES, BEFORE BEING HEALED

Christ in us. Why? So we don't act like Christ. So we stop loving. We simply can't love others well if we hate ourselves.

My soul had been broken and needed to be touched by the Greatest Love in this universe. Few could detect my true opinion of myself because I was quite secretive about it. I was saying all the right stuff to cover up all the wrong stuff on the inside. Yet all the while, I was screaming for someone to help me feel like me again.

I learned that night at youth camp that I had to be healed of self-hatred first, before I could ever be healed of my physical issues. Those bad thoughts had been distorting the real me, but the real me was more determined than ever to let God's love rule.

I started trying to live more from the inside out instead of from the outside in. I made daily conscious decisions to accept God's love for me, and He began to pour acceptance into my soul. I learned to recognize the downward spiral of negative emotions and thoughts that would lead to hating myself. Then I would make the conscious decision to fight self-hatred with my words. It was a process, for sure.

I continued to fight physical pain, but at least the emotional battle was getting better.

MEDICAL MERRY-GO-ROUND

Still, I had no diagnosis. After a year with one doctor who tried hormone therapies, thinking there was a link between some female problems I was having and the enlargement of my stomach, he sent me to another doctor. She took a "wait-and-see" attitude, but felt strongly that it was a body shape or muscle imbalance issue. Several times I wanted to look for other doctors, because I wanted real answers, but I felt a strong warning, a loud, "No!" on the inside. I think at that point I was still really afraid, and fear was seeking an answer. But God was trying to get me off of the medical merry-go-round so I could do things differently.

One lady recently asked me why I didn't "get on top of the illness sooner," but it's not that I didn't try to get a diagnosis. I tried four different doctors. Each time, I was brushed off or told to "wait and see how it progresses." *Maybe God was protecting me from hearing too much. He wanted me to trust Him.*

At the beginning of 2008, I followed through with some prescribed physical therapy on a weekly basis, doing specific stretches to alleviate pain and loosen my incredibly tight connective core muscles. My doctor said perhaps some of this was a result of the childhood car accident. Although PT and stretching helped my muscles temporarily, it just seemed that my stomach stayed the same or got worse.

After a few months of sessions, the therapist told me I should probably never jog or do any high-impact cardio again because my spine had no shock absorption due to lack of curve. I was stunned. I felt trapped in my own body. It was enough to send me into a fresh bout of hopelessness. Once again, I was tempted to look in the mirror and number all the things I hated about myself. But instead, I ran to Jesus and poured out my tears and my pain to Him.

On top of meeting with a physical therapist, I got a prescription for therapeutic massage, and so I started doing that every other week. One day, halfway through my massage, I told my massage therapist it was just too painful for me to lie on my stomach for very long. I told her I'd have to turn over to my back.

She seemed concerned and examined my spine. She said, "Have you ever had x-rays of your back? It looks like you have lack of curve in your lower back. And your vertebra down here are sticking out! The lordosis of your spine is wrong."

The words of that first doctor came echoing back. ***"This is probably just the way you are. The way your body is built."***

A PARTNER FOR THE FIGHT

In September of 2008, the church had grown and was looking for a person to manage operations. I was on a panel of directors doing interviews for that position, and one night they brought in a guy from Texas. I contributed a few tough questions during his interview, and we all decided he had a good head on his shoulders. Jason Freudiger was hired.

I tease him now that I gave him the job because I thought he was cute. (In reality, it was our H.R. department that made the decision to hire him, but don't tell him that. Haha!)

As I got to know Jason, I discovered that he was passionate, full of vision, kind, and loyal. He, too, had overcome many things in his life, and he was familiar with keeping faith during dark personal times. Originally from Texas, he had moved to Florida and now to Ohio, so he teases that he's a "missionary to the north." He doesn't love cold weather, but it turns out he loved me.

As our friendship turned to love, he accepted and loved me for who I was, and he never said anything to make me feel anything but perfect. Our relationship was easy and comfortable and fun. It wasn't hard to enjoy life when I was around him.

We were married on September 20, 2009. What a sweet day!

CELEBRATING OUR WEDDING DAY IN A DRESS THAT ALMOST HID MY STOMACH

What a wonderful feeling to know that I now had a partner for life.

Everything was beautiful. But then the physical problems took an ugly turn for the worse.

On our honeymoon cruise, just days after we said, "I do," I started vomiting, shaking, and feeling like my organs were on fire. My back and spine hurt so bad. Jason called the cruise doctor, and they wheeled me into the sick bay. I was semi-conscious as they determined I had developed a bacterial infection.

The E.R. doctor on board our cruise ship asked Jason some familiar questions. "Is she pregnant? Her stomach is protruding quite a bit. Is it always like that?" I was too sick to explain why my body looked like it did. They quickly did a pregnancy test, which came back negative, before administering strong rounds of intravenous medications as Jason held my hand. It was a scary night for my groom and for me.

Within a few days, the infection was gone. But fear held its grip.

A month into our newlywed life, I suddenly started experiencing nausea and stomach pain on a daily basis. I couldn't eat anything without feeling sick. Of course, I took more pregnancy tests just in case, but all were negative. Most of the time, I didn't tell Jason how bad I really felt, but he would constantly ask me, "Are you okay?"

We had just moved into a rental house, I had new responsibilities at home, I worked full-time, and I did not have time to deal with this! I tried prebiotics, probiotics, antacids, and anything else I thought might help. I kept Rolaids, peppermints, and ginger with me at all times to try and fight the nausea.

On our first Christmas as a couple, we went to my parents' house for our traditional Christmas Eve dinner, but I felt too sick to eat anything. Miserable, I eventually just flopped down in the other room, missing out on the good conversation and delicious food. My favorite meal of the year is my mom's eggs Benedict on Christmas morning, but once again, I could only eat a few bites before feeling terrible. I was getting so tired of coping.

Jason took me to my regular doctor that week. She recommended prescription medication, saying, "Some people just have chronic acid problems and they live on meds. Try the medication and see if it helps you cope. If not, we can try something stronger that will take away the nausea," she said. I asked her if she thought it had anything to do with my distended abdomen, but she was convinced that my spine was the cause of my body shape. I felt like she didn't truly listen. Recently, I discovered that all of those symptoms lined up with having displaced organs due to cysts or tumors.

I did not want to deal with another "chronic" issue! I didn't want to be on medication for the rest of my life. I decided not to fill the prescription and instead limited myself to a bland diet. *This is ridiculous!* I thought to myself. *I'm 25 years old! I should be enjoying life with my new husband!*

A few months later, in early March, 2010, my dad was invited to speak at a conference that focused on emotional, mental, and physical healing; and I felt like I needed to go. We prayed and decided to believe God that I was going to come back from that conference completely free of this pain and nausea in my stomach. While I couldn't picture being free of everything, I could believe God to heal this one problem. I would start there.

After sitting through three days of services full of hope and Truth from the Bible, I could feel faith rising up on the inside. My friend was there, and she prayed for me at the end of that service. From that moment on, ALL the nausea and digestion issues stopped completely. We went out to eat after that service, and as I took the first bite, I said, "I believe that I am healed." And I felt no more nausea from then on!

Even though my body was still disfigured and my abdomen was still so large, I started being able to eat without fear. I had won a small battle, and I realized that I was onto something. It sparked real hope in my heart that things could change.

When I got back in town, Jason and I found the cutest little fixer-upper cottage in a quaint town just outside of Columbus. God made a way for us to purchase it with cash, and we were so excited!

But just then, I suffered another physical blow. We were within a week of closing on our new house when I became very ill. I had a high fever for several days, so we went to an urgent care center. The doctor said I had a respiratory infection and gave me an antibiotic.

I started taking it, but three days later, I

could not get out of bed. The real problem continued to rage in my body. It was the sickest I had ever been in my life up to that point. I found myself too weak to walk. I was in so much pain I couldn't stand, and so delirious I could barely talk. My hands were turning blue and I was shaking so violently from the fever, Jason had to carry me to the car and rush me to the emergency room.

For the second time in my brand-new marriage, I found myself in the hospital, on strong antibiotics. They found the real problem—pyelonephritis, a severe kidney infection. Knowing what I know now about the condition of my body, I also had every sign of hydronephrosis (blockage and swelling of the kidneys due to pressure being put on them). By now, I was also severely dehydrated. Then, I was allergic to the prescription they put me on, so I had almost every side effect on the bottle—including hypoglycemic blood sugar swings, swollen tongue, dizziness, and nausea. Not fun.

We had to be out of our rental and into our new cottage by the end of the next week. I focused on regaining strength and forcing myself to eat protein every two hours to keep my blood sugar high enough, while Jason scrambled to prep for moving. I remember my wonderful family coming over and helping Jason do all the work, while I lay there and told them where things went.

A few months later, I suffered another kidney infection, again accompanied by fever, weakness, nausea, and that required bed-rest. At least this time I recognized the symptoms soon enough to catch it early. During the day, I stayed at my parents' house while Jason went to work so someone could keep an eye on me. I was so weak. Several times, I collapsed on the floor and had to call my mom for help. More medication. More medical bills. Doctors were beginning to comment that the frequency of infection didn't seem normal and they weren't sure where it could be stemming from. Satan was fighting hard to steal the bud of hope that had begun earlier that March.

When I was strong enough, Jason and I started pouring our effort into making our new house a home, and I tried not to complain about my physical problems.

I had the suspicion that whatever was causing issues with my abdomen was also causing problems with organs functioning well, perhaps promoting an environment in which infections could propagate.

CONNECTING TO THE ANSWER

Let me give you a little insight into my mind-set at the time. All throughout the years of fear and pain, I knew that God still healed people, yet I couldn't see myself healed. I knew God was more powerful than this problem, but I was powerless to connect to His solutions for my body. If you had asked me during those years, "Does

God still heal people like the stories in the Bible say?" I would have told you, "Yes! Absolutely!" I'm sure a skeptic could have replied, "Well then, why aren't you healed?" Good question. We will get to that and we will get back to my story in a moment.

First, let me give you an illustration. One day a woman called a customer service center complaining that her brand-new, state-of-the-art computer would not turn on anymore. "I keep hitting the power button, but the thing won't turn on," she complained. "I can't believe you sold me a piece of junk!"

The customer service representative asked a few questions and walked her through some troubleshooting steps, to no avail. Then he asked, "Ma'am, this may sound like a silly question, but can you please check that the power cord is plugged in properly?"

"You think I'm stupid?"

"Just please check the power source to humor me, Ma'am."

Long pause. "Oh...it is unplugged," she sheepishly replied.

There was nothing wrong with the computer, and there was nothing wrong with the electricity in the outlet; but until she plugged in the cord, nothing was going to happen. There was a disconnect.

That was my problem. Quite simply, there was a disconnect between my head and my heart. I had a lot of great theology in my head, but my heart was unplugged from the Source of Power. My disconnect stemmed from several things that I want to show you later on (the greatest of which was an identity issue caused by the self-hatred I battled earlier in my twenties).

If you or I were the child of an influential billionaire, there would be certain perks, special access, and great influence that would come along with our position in the family. Being God's child comes with all that and more! But we have to know we are in the family. As I sought God in that first year of marriage, He began to illuminate my identity as His child and what that meant. I still struggled to believe what God said about my identity and worth, thus I didn't believe what He said about my health, either.

I wanted to be well, but I was sick. There was a disconnect I couldn't seem to reconcile.

Many people experience a disconnect between what they want and what they have.

It is said that the biggest gap in the world is the gap between knowing and doing. If we all did what we know to do, we would all be skinny, rich, and happy. I will add that there can also be a gap between knowing (head knowledge) and believing (heart knowledge). And without believing, we will never act on faith. And in fact, God cannot "do" without first our "knowing" and then our "believing." Why? God has given humans free will. That means He has limited Himself to what we allow Him to do in our lives.

The connecting factor of faith in God is what allows Him to act on our behalves.

Faith is what joins us to God's power, much like an electric cord joins a lamp to a power source. What is faith? Faith is believing with absolute certainty. It is being in total agreement with someone. It is being fully convinced of something. When we are in total agreement with what God said, and we believe with certainty that it's true for us, we can have what we agree with Him on. If we don't remain fully convinced and in agreement with God, there will be a disconnect.

Recently, I had a young man come up to me and say, "I've been angry at God for a long time because my dad died of cancer, and he was a pastor. He said he believed God could heal him. He still died. But I think I'm beginning to understand why. He was afraid of the cancer. I don't think he believed Jesus could heal him. Perhaps he allowed fear to overcome his faith."

It's a tough truth to own, but oftentimes when we see a discrepancy between God's promises and what we actually have in our own lives, it's because there's a disconnect between what we know and what we truly believe. It is not because God changed His mind or "shut off" His power. It's because we haven't plugged in the power cord! Wishful thinking will not connect us to God's power source. Saying, "I hope God helps me," won't do a thing, because hope can't connect us to God's power source. It says in Hebrews 11:6 (NLT):

It is impossible to please God without faith. Anyone who wants to come to him must believe that God exists and that he rewards those who sincerely seek him.

Sometimes, in the midst of experiencing symptoms and hearing fearful reports, it is hard for a sick person to put their full confidence in God. People lose the will to live. They lose hope. They grow weary in the fight. They disconnect from the Power Source. They may not even realize it, because they can still be saying the right things to others but believing something different on the inside. I know all that from experience. Someone can say to their family member, "Yes, I want to live," but they've already given up the will to live in their heart.

We can't always tell the difference between what someone says and what they actually believe. Only God knows what's in the heart of a person. The point is, we can't blame God for the pain and suffering we see around us. Know that He is only good. It wasn't His fault I was sick. As my dad says, "The problem must be on our end, because it's not on God's end!"

In other words, I was still lacking some knowledge and understanding in how to connect with God's answer. When we find ourselves in a situation that isn't getting better, that's when we must cry, "God, help my unbelief! Show me what I need to do! Change me, God!"

Some people argue that a Healer must not exist because there is so much pain and sickness in the world. I would ask them this: Just because there are people with terribly rotted teeth, does that mean dentists don't exist? No! It just means that those people with bad teeth haven't gone to the dentist and received dental care. It's the same with healing. Just because there are people who are sick doesn't mean that a Healer doesn't exist. It just means that the sick people haven't gone to God and received healing.

I certainly do not say any of this to make anyone feel bad for going through hard things. I don't want anyone to feel condemned or as if they just aren't doing everything right, as if they aren't following some mystical formula. (Faith isn't a formula, by the way.) I understand there is a very real spiritual fight between health and sickness, between faith and fear—and it takes courage and determination to stay in that fight. I say all this because I, too, was talking the talk but not walking the walk.

Every time I tried to believe God for a miracle during those years of sickness, I would experience a faith killer—something to disappoint and discourage me. Whether it was a hurtful comment from someone or another symptom, a battle with self-hatred or a report from a doctor, I couldn't seem to hold on to faith in God for healing. You could say I was a "heart hypocrite." I was caught between two realities: the one the Bible promised and the one my body was experiencing. I couldn't seem to reconcile the two.

Throughout my early twenties, I was what the Bible calls "double-minded" and "unstable in all my ways" (James 1:8) because one day I would believe I could get better and the next day I would sink into despair.

If I would have been honest with myself, I wasn't fully convinced that I could get better, because I had such a strong picture of being flawed and disfigured. *Damaged goods.*

I finally realized that I had to overshadow the wrong beliefs with the right ones from God's Word. I had to send biblical promises, like weapons, into my internal war to fight the lies I had allowed to invade my heart.

I began to fast and pray, asking God what else I needed to fix on my end to receive my complete healing. And He told me.

FORGIVENESS

Back at that youth camp encounter, I had started the battle to love myself as a person and to reclaim my identity. God now began to show me that physical health is just a part of what makes a person whole. Emotional health is so key to being truly well! My emotions still needed healed in deeper ways. I wanted to be healthy, but I really needed to be emotionally whole first. Physical health was part of the restoration of identity I would walk through, but first had to come emotional health. Being emotionally healthy means being at peace with yourself and with others. And I wasn't.

God showed me my next step: I needed to forgive the people who had done malicious things to me, who had gossiped against me, who had made me feel less beautiful or worthy than them. And most importantly, I had to let go of the words they had spoken against me. You see, people had said hurtful things along the journey. There had been personal attacks against me from those who were in dark places themselves.

Hurting people hurt people. And if we are going to live this life, at some point or another someone is going to hurt us. People had said I wasn't this or that. Some had made me feel less than good enough, whether intentionally or not. And I was still living with the doubts those words and actions had inflicted. *I wasn't confident in myself because of some of those experiences.*

Now God was challenging me to forgive them and forget those words. *But how can I forget what they said?* I thought. God answered back, "By putting more weight in what I say about you." It was time to stop living in the words of my critics. The doubts generated from those words were actually causing me to fulfill their predictions and make them true!

I had to get my courage and self-confidence back. I started spending more time worshiping in the presence of the Great I Am, because He made me feel great just being around Him.

It says in Hebrews 4:16:

Let us then approach God's throne of grace with confidence, so that we may receive mercy and find grace to help us in our time of need.

In order to receive my healing, I had to regain my confidence. Unforgiveness, self-pity, a victim mentality, and martyrdom syndrome will steal boldness faster than you can say, "Woe is me!" My personality is more laid back and "go with the flow," so it's easy for me to hand the reins of my life over to someone else if I'm not careful. It's easy for me to be overly concerned about other people's opinions. I can readily take a backseat to what other people want and shove my true wants and desires into hiding.

Now I had to take a stand against the enemy for what was rightfully mine. I had to find the confidence to take the reins back, to stop living in the past or in the shadows.

It was time to start living like a secure daughter of the King.

I let go of the hurt. I stopped being a victim. I started truly loving and praying for the people who had wounded me in the past. I was at peace with them in my heart. In fact, I wanted to do something nice for each of them! Someone once said that bitterness is like drinking poison and hoping it hurts the other person, when, in fact, it's only going to kill YOU.

Looking back, many of those people may not have known they had hurt me. It probably wasn't intentional. I don't know, and it doesn't really matter. There are people I have hurt, too, so I had to forgive myself for my mistakes. No one is perfect—we all sin and fall short.

I started praying, "Jesus, help me to have the same power to forgive myself and others that you had when you were on the cross and you said about your murderers, 'Father forgive them, for they do not know what they are doing'" (Luke 23:34a).

Forgiveness was part of the healing on the inside that had to happen before I could ever see healing on the outside. It was a healing I won through months of letting God's love change my emotions. I journaled my thoughts, prayers, and feelings, asking

God to help me renew my mind to His reality.

I had to believe what He believed about me in order to receive what He had already given to me.

DECEPTIVE REALITY

We can't judge the validity of God's Word based on someone else's experience. We can't judge God's existence based on our senses. Our senses can lie. What we perceive as reality can be deceiving; what we see with our natural eyes is not always the truth. We, as humans, cannot see the motives and the intents of people's hearts as God can. We see a situation and make a decision based on the evidence we have. However, that conclusion may not be accurate.

People used to believe the earth was flat based on the evidence they had at the time. If you've ever seen an illusionist or magician, you know that our senses can be tricked.

That is why we cannot judge situations based on our emotions or physical senses.

When we place more trust in human emotions or experiences than we do in God, we are doomed for disappointment and failure. I've heard people say, "Well, Brother So-and-So was a good man who believed in healing and he died of a heart attack. So I don't believe God heals everyone," or, "If God is good then why did my sister die of breast cancer?"

Listen, my own lack of faith was NOT an indication of God's lack of power.

It was an indication of my heart condition, my messed up thinking about myself, and my lack of knowledge.

Our situations and senses can try to make us believe the negative stimuli around us is Truth, but we have to become confident that God's Truth is found in His Word, and that's how we will live our lives. God can't lie, and all of His promises are "Yes" for those who believe. Numbers 23:19

says, "God is not human, that he should lie, not a human being, that he should change his mind. Does he speak and then not act? Does he promise and not fulfill?"

If He promises health, it's not a maybe. It's always a "Yes!" In 2 Corinthians 1:20 it says:

> For no matter how many promises God has made, they are "Yes" in Christ. And so through him the "Amen" is spoken by us to the glory of God.

Notice that WE are the ones who have to say "Amen"—which simply means "so be it unto me"—to what God has already promised. So the conversation could go like this:

Me: "God, do you want to heal me?"

God: "Yes! Jesus demonstrated my will for humankind. He healed all who were oppressed of the devil (Acts 10:38)."

Me: "Okay! Because you can't lie, I believe that your 'Yes' is the Truth. Now I say I'll have that. So be it unto me!"

Romans 3:4 says, "...Let God be true, and every human being a liar...." There will always be people who doubt God's Word, or who try to make it more complicated than it is. There will always be lies perpetuated by satan to our culture and even to churches. He is the father of all lies and there is no truth in him. Jesus said this about satan in John 8:44b:

> He was a murderer from the beginning, not holding to the truth, for there is no truth in him. When he lies, he speaks his native language, for he is a liar and the father of lies.

There will always be bad things in this world because, just like there is a good God, there is an evil devil, and his mission is to destroy humans (John 10:10). Why does satan hate us? Because God loves us, and satan is God's enemy. Therefore, he is our enemy, too. He will cause us pain if we allow him in our lives. He wants to murder humans. But he can't do that unless we legally give him a right to come into our lives.

Our enemy doesn't make bad choices or wrong patterns of thinking *appear* as if they are the road to death, even though they are. He makes them seem good, pleasurable, normal—reality. Satan is an illusionist. He is really good at getting humans to believe a lie (John 8:44). That's how he got mankind to disobey God in the first place. (Read Genesis 3!) That is why we must constantly compare our lifestyles and patterns of thinking with God's standards and Word.

I know now that I once believed lies about myself ("This is just the way you are. You'll always be this way. You're just broken.") All the while, I was saying I believed in healing. I led worship for my church and lived as good a life as I could, but I was just keeping up appearances on the outside while satan was eating me alive on the inside.

Outwardly, it would've appeared I was "doing everything right." But what was coming out of my mouth and what was in my heart were two different things. Now, don't tell me that you've never said something you didn't believe! That's where I was, saying one thing but believing another. I would say, "I am healed," but what I really believed was, "This is the way I am and always will be." My *mental picture* of who I was and how I looked had to change.

THE X-RAYS

I finally went to a new doctor who did some x-rays; and when I saw those x-rays, I saw the inside of the body that had hurt for nine years.

He showed me on the x-rays where I had indeed lost curvature in my lower back, and where some of the lower vertebra seemed pushed outward, out of place. It looked like something inside there was pushing out on all of my bones. And there it was—a large, cloudy mass in my abdomen. So it wasn't just the normal shape of my body or my spine, like other doctors had suggested. There was definitely something in there, and it was growing.

When I saw that x-ray, I finally could see the internal picture causing the outward physical issues. My intestines were pushed up into my rib cage, much like a pregnant woman's. My organs were overcrowded. Nerves were being pinched.

The doctor walked me through these observations. He said that specialists would need consulted. But he was also a Christian and reminded me that God was more than able to heal this situation.

When I saw those x-rays, I had a choice. *What do I do now, Lord?* I thought. *Should I run to another specialist? What if I have to have a serious surgery? What if by removing the growth they have to remove other organs? What if I need a hysterectomy?*

My mother had experienced an ovarian cyst in her younger years, and my mind raced to that possibility. I started thinking about my dream of having children. *What if...?* No! I wasn't going to let myself think about the what ifs.

After talking it over with my husband, we agreed to not make an appointment to see another doctor just yet. I knew I had to fight off this fear first. By the way, never make a decision when you are fighting fear. Wait to hear God's leading. Get in a place of peace and confidence. When you are listening to fear, you will follow every suggestion but God's, and you will make poor decisions.

As I prayed about the problem that night, I absentmindedly flipped through some photo albums. Photographs of Jason and myself as babies looked back at me, and suddenly, my lifelong desire to be a mother came crashing into my heart. Tears sprung to my eyes at the intensity of these emotions. Jason and I had just celebrated our first anniversary, and we were ready for a family. But in the back of my mind, I had worried about this health issue, knowing it would make it very difficult to carry a baby, perhaps even impossible. Would I ever hold my own precious little one in my arms?

God, I don't want to give up my dream of having children, I thought.

"You don't have to," I heard God whisper to my heart.

Those words from God, like wind lifting a kite off the ground, suddenly bolstered my courage. The will to fight rose up inside of me. *No!* I would not lie down and allow satan to steal my future anymore! Enough! I would not mourn the loss of *anything* because all was not lost. The only one who was going to lose was going to be satan. I stood up, wiped the tears from my eyes, and

I prayed (or rather shouted) a "Hannah's prayer." (See 1 Samuel 1 and 2.)

Hannah was a woman in the Bible who was childless for years until she cried out to God, and He healed her. She gave birth to the mighty prophet Samuel a year after her prayer.

I cried out to God that night and said, "Lord, I want to be healed before I get pregnant. I want to be able to have children. I will raise them to serve you all the days of their lives, and I will cherish and love them. I dedicate them to you right now, and I believe you can heal my body so that I can carry children and carry them without pain. And I'm going to do whatever it takes to get rid of the unbelief in my heart. No matter what, I'm going to fight this fear and win my victory!"

I decided I was going to be healed of it all, from head to toe. I didn't want to simply keep dealing with symptoms. I made a decision that it was over.

Sometimes I think we just need to have determination. We need to have "whatever-it-takes" kind of faith, like Hannah did. And like the men in the story I'm about to tell you.

Mark 2 tells the story of four men who were trying to take their paralyzed friend to Jesus for prayer, but they could not get past the crowds into the house where Jesus taught. Instead of giving up or getting angry, they made a way! They climbed on top of the house, tore a hole in the roof, and lowered their friend right down in front of Jesus! That is definitely whatever-it-takes kind of faith. Here's what happened:

> Then they lowered the man on his mat, right down in front of Jesus. Seeing their faith, Jesus said to the paralyzed man, "My child, your sins are forgiven."

But that's not all! It goes on to say:

Then Jesus turned to the paralyzed man and said, "Stand up, pick up your mat, and go home!" And the man jumped up, grabbed his mat, and walked out through the stunned onlookers. They were all amazed and praised God, exclaiming, "We've never seen anything like this before!" (Mark 2:4b, 10b-12, NLT).

I now felt the same determination those men had. It was the desperate determination for change.

I tried to picture what my body, my spine, and my stomach should look like. Then I felt the Holy Spirit instruct me to start praying against the growth that was affecting my organs. God knew exactly what was wrong, and He was telling me how to pray. It made complete sense that a tumor or cyst was what was putting pressure on my muscles, spine, and organs—and it had to go! I pictured that thing gone in my mind.

"Would it have been wrong for you to go to a doctor for surgery?" someone once asked me. No, but the thought of doing that made me so fearful. I had to do what I had peace about in that moment of my life.

I believe God can use doctors to do wonderful things. He made our bodies to heal themselves in many ways, and doctors can help our bodies down that road. Ultimately, doctors simply help someone's body do what God created it to do. He placed the wisdom for cures in men. If it were up to satan, there would be no cures and no doctors. So doctors are doing good things, and God uses doctors. **But God is not limited to using doctors**, and His power is more than able to replace body parts, mend broken bones, remove tumors and cancers, and heal us in every way, without human intervention.

Ultimately, the Bible says God will provide a way of escape out of temptation (1 Corinthians 10:13), and that includes the temptation to give in to fear. So if we have peace about seeing a doctor or having some form of procedure done, we should follow that peace. If we build up our faith enough to be able to picture healing without medical intervention, all the better.

Maybe God will lead us to a combination of the two, much like a pastor friend of ours who was diagnosed with cancer and decided to have the cancerous tumor removed but did not have chemo or radiation. Instead, he went on a strict cleansing diet, and he was 100% cancer free a year later.

It's up to our faith to determine what we can picture being possible. For me, I knew I had more faith for healing apart from medical intervention than I had faith for a medical intervention to go well and fix the problem.

That weekend at Faith Life Church, my father (whom I affectionately call "Pastor Dad") started teaching a series on healing called, "Live Whole: God's Healthcare

Plan." It was perfect timing, and after the service I knew I wanted to believe God for healing, without any surgery. Jason agreed.

Through the next weeks of sitting through the healing teachings at church, I heard many scriptures from the Bible (which I've included at the end of this book). I heard many testimonies from people who had been healed by God despite impossible odds. I started getting excited! Fear started turning to faith. I started seeing what was "normal" to God, and it wasn't sickness.

I realized satan had tricked me into accepting sickness as my "normal."

God didn't make me like this! I had simply accepted what that first doctor had told me, that this was just the way I was, that I would have to live with this. And I had taken the bait, hook, line, and sinker.

I had allowed satan to move in and set up camp in my mind and my body. I had let him trespass on my territory. My body is God's temple, His property (1 Corinthians

6:19-20), and I had allowed sickness to stay for too long. It was time to kick it out.

I was tired of the embarrassment. I was tired of pain. I was tired of being tired. And finally, I saw that I didn't have to live like this any longer.

The facts were saying I was sick still, but God's Truth said I was healed.

FACTS VS. TRUTH

There's a big difference between facts and Truth. Science and circumstances speak facts. God speaks Truth. He is bigger than any physical evidence, any sickness, or disease. Our facts can come from a doctor, but our truth must be from God's Truth alone. Period.

You see, I had accepted the problem as truth—MY truth. But it was just a fact that could be changed by Truth. When the Truth and facts don't line up, we have a role to play to bring the two into alignment or agreement with one another. Let me explain.

Many times the physical realm does not line up with the spiritual realm of heaven. It's our job to bring them back into alignment, using our faith as the "heavy machinery" and the Word of God as the measuring standard.

Jesus said it this way in Matthew 17:20 (NLT):

> "You don't have enough faith," Jesus told them. "I tell you the truth, if you had faith even as small as a mustard seed, you could say to this mountain, 'Move from here to there,' and it would move. Nothing would be impossible."

What does it mean to bring the physical into alignment with the supernatural—with heaven? Let me illustrate with a scenario.

One day you tell your children they

are not allowed to play in the street because you know it will harm them. But then your 15-year-old goes out and starts skateboarding on a busy road. The truth is, you, as a parent, do not allow nor condone that dangerous behavior. The fact is, your teenager is breaking your rules and playing in the road. You step outside your house and yell, "Get out of the road right now! You are not allowed to play there!"

Your teenager wants to show they are grown up enough to make their own decisions, so they continue to break your rules. You yell once again, "If you love me, get out of the road!" This time, your child reluctantly moves out of the road and just in time. A drunk driver in a truck roars around the curve and surely would have killed your child if they had disobeyed your command for another moment.

What happened? Your words brought your child into alignment with your will for his life, but that child had to choose to act on your words. Your will was not for your child to be killed by a truck, nor were you "allowing" it. Your son had stepped outside of your will, outside the boundaries of protection.

Perhaps your neighbors had been watching your son playing in the freeway, and saying, "I can't believe she allows her kid to skateboard on this four-lane road! She's obviously a bad parent." But that's not the truth. The fact that your child was breaking your rules, as a parent, did not make you a bad parent. Your child has a free will and was simply exerting that will against your will. When you spoke those words and your child finally decided to act upon them, the truth about your will and your child's behavior *came into alignment.*

God has spoken His will through Jesus. He has also set up spiritual principles and natural laws in the earth for our benefit. He is trying to tell us about these principles. But are we listening? Are we living in them? Are we diligently learning them? And beyond that, are we also speaking God's will over our lives? Are we echoing heaven's will for our lives, bringing heaven to earth?

When we finally start to act on God's Word and then speak those same Words with authority, physical matter changes! Mountains move! The natural realm lines up with heaven's reality.

The behavior of our bodies will come into alignment with the Truth of God's will for us.

God is a good dad, a good parent, and He does not want us to die. But we are the ones who must obey His words and bring Truth and facts, heaven and earth, into alignment. We have to bring His Kingdom laws to bear upon our circumstances. We have to live under the rules of heaven even though we live on earth—they apply here, too! Just like your will for your child applied inside the house as much as it did outside the house, God's will for us applies here on earth as much as it does in heaven.

There should be no discrepancy between God's authority in our lives while we are residing here than when we will be residing in heaven one day.

Sure, we have to fight our worldly desires and sinful cravings, but the Truth, as demonstrated in Jesus's life, is the gold standard either way. We can base our theology on Jesus's life. He came to show us God's parenting choices. He only did what He saw Father God doing, thus demonstrating His will to us. By the way, He doesn't change His mind like we earthly parents do! He is constant, faithful, and trustworthy.

Let me share an example of heaven coming to earth as exemplified in my friend's life. During the first week of the "Live Whole" teachings my dad was doing at our church, my friend Amy shared her story. She said she had been having debilitating daily migraine headaches. They were so bad she had to get weekly injections in her skull to deal with the pain. She had to sit at home in a dark room, not being able to enjoy her newlywed life with her husband. When there was no hope for curing the problem, she had reached the end of her rope. But that's when she reached up for God. She looked in her Bible to see what God's will was for her health. She found Romans 8:11 (KJV):

> But if the Spirit of him that raised up Jesus from the dead dwell in you, ***he that raised up Christ from the dead shall also quicken your mortal bodies by his Spirit that dwelleth in you*** (emphasis mine).

The dictionary says that word *quicken* means "to come to life, or revive"; and *revive* means "to make (someone or something) strong, healthy, or active again." In other words, Amy realized her body could be restored to its original state of vigor, health, and activity, without pain.

After Amy prayed with her husband, she said the migraine headaches completely stopped. Doctors had no explanation. She was totally set free from the vice grip of pain!

When I heard my friend's story, I grabbed hold of it. I, too, wanted my REAL body back, the way God intended! I wanted restored.

I decided I needed to start bombarding my mind with God's Word until all doubt was gone, until I was convinced that it was God's will to heal me. I didn't run to the altar to be prayed for that first weekend. I knew I needed to wait until my heart was *convinced* it was God's desire for me to live whole, and *then* I could be prayed for to be healed, as James 5:14-15 says to do:

> Is anyone among you sick? Let them call for the elders of the church to pray over them and anoint them

with oil in the name of the Lord. And the prayer offered in faith will make the sick person well; and the Lord will raise them up....

My mind had been warped by the pain and by the physical disfigurement I saw in the mirror every single day. Now I had to picture myself healed and normal. I had to see with my spirit eyes what I would look like and feel like as a totally **whole** human being. I realized my body was made special:

Do you not know that your body is a **temple of the Holy Spirit**, who is in you, whom you have received from God? You are not your own; you were bought at a price. Therefore **honor God with your bodies**" (1 Corinthians 6:19-20, emphasis mine).

GOD'S WILL

…how God anointed Jesus of Nazareth with the Holy Spirit and power, and how he went around doing good and *healing all* who were under the power of the devil, because God was with him (Acts 10:38, emphasis mine).

That last scripture doesn't say that Jesus healed some people. It says He healed them all—you and I are part of *all!* Jesus never turned to a sick person and said, "I am not going to heal you because this sickness is meant to teach you a lesson." **When someone asked Jesus for healing, He never said no.**

We can draw the conclusion then that it is not God's will for us to suffer with sickness. Sure, we *can* learn things through physical suffering, but we don't *have* to learn that way. It's not God's will for us to learn that way, just like it would not have been your will that your son learn not to play in the road by being hit by the truck. God is good, and only good things can come from Him. We are human beings with our own free wills, living in a fallen world full of evil, fighting an enemy named satan who wants to take us out if we will let him.

God doesn't give people sickness to teach them something, nor does He "allow" it. Humans are the ones who allowed evil in this earth. And if we belong to Jesus, with the Covenant He gave us on the cross, then we are the only ones who put up with sickness in our bodies. We don't wish for it, but satan will try to bring stuff against us. Then he will try to blame it on God, our one and only source of power against him.

If we are God's children, we already have every good thing God has, if we will only believe that simple Truth. But maybe someone in your church has said, "Well, our human definition of *good* and God's definition of *good* are different. God allows some things we might call bad because He knows they will actually be good for us in the end. How can we know what good and bad really are?" Let's talk about that. Of course, a wicked person's definition of "good" can be degenerate, but if you are born again to God, then your spirit is alive to God's will. God's Holy Spirit is inside of you, and you can know what is good. You can also know God's will. It doesn't have to be a mystery!

You have a God-given conscience to discern good from evil. You have the Holy Spirit, who is your Counselor. You have "the mind of Christ" (1 Corinthians 2:16). You can know the very thoughts of God, according to that scripture! Your God-given conscience knows good from evil. I think you have a pretty good idea of what's beautiful, pleasing, right, good, and just. You especially do if you spend time with God. When you spend time with someone, you get to know what they do and don't like. You start to understand what they call good and bad.

So then, tell me how on earth we can call cancer, blindness, or the death of a child "good"? It doesn't feel right in our hearts to say that's good. It doesn't sit well with our consciences. It doesn't come from God, that's why!

Some bad things happen in this world because of the evil inside human hearts. Violence, racism, abuse, adultery, neglect, slander, gossip, and lack are caused by humans under the influence of satan's lies. Evil is the absence of God, and when people don't allow God into their lives, they can act violently, ruthlessly, greedily, lustfully, fearfully, and viciously. Free will was the greatest gift and also the greatest responsibility He gave humans.

Now, God is so good that He will still bring us good things in the midst of fighting a bad situation. But that doesn't mean it originates from Him. If you've lost a loved one or had terrible things done to you or you've lost some battles in your life,

don't feel discouraged or condemned—
God is still working to bring good from
that bad situation! He's still fighting on
your behalf. And He never condemns you
or me. He simply keeps on loving us. He's
the perfect parent!

Using a parenting example again,
imagine your child has a bicycle. It's his
prized possession, and he rides it every day.
Imagine you are a multimillionaire with
much influence in your city, and because
of that you have a lot of enemies. One day,
your child rides into a section of town you
warned him about. A thug hired by one
of your enemies sees his chance as your
child rides down a dark alley! He comes
and pushes your child off his bike, roughs
him up, threatens him, and then steals his
bicycle.

When your child comes limping back
to your house, bruised and crying, would
you say: "Oh, what a wonderful thing to
have happen! This is good for you! You've

not been 100% obedient lately, so I'm going to allow that thug to get away with this. Through this you can learn the lesson of forgiveness"? Um, NOT!

A good parent would react in a compassionate, caring way. I know what I would do in that situation: I would grab my child in a big bear hug, bandage his wounds, and then buy him a bicycle that is better than the old one! And then I would use my power and influence to bring that thug to justice. You see, I, as a parent, just brought good out of an evil situation. My child got a better bike than his old one. I didn't *cause or allow* the evil, though.

MY 30-DAY DARE

Let me say it again: we can know God's will for our lives through Jesus's example. Reading about Jesus's life brings clarity and faith in the midst of all the voices we hear in life. During the weeks after I received that initial set of x-rays, I took something I called my "30-day healing dare." I felt the Holy Spirit daring me to saturate my life with His Truth. I took 30 days and shut off every voice that had fear, death, or destruction, including TV, radio, magazines, and other reading material.

I spent 30 days speaking 30 healing scriptures out loud at least three times daily. I would then follow those up with declarations over my body. And I sat in on three services every weekend at my church where my dad was teaching, "Live Whole!"

I would go home and say, *"Body, you will respond to the Word of God that you've just heard. Pain, you were defeated by Jesus, and you have no right to remain in my body. Tumor, I command you to die at the roots. Spine, I command you to be curved and without pain."* This focused attention on the Bible helped me become convinced that healing applied to my situation.

Television advertisements and programs are often full of fear, sickness, and death; so I turned that off. I closed off all the distractions. I fasted from social media and the Internet except for work-related usage. I was determined to flood every cell of my being with Truth. ***Negativity is a life killer, so I carefully guarded my eyes and ears to only let in positive things.***

Faith (agreement with God) only comes one way: hearing the Word of God until it becomes bigger in our hearts than the problem (Romans 10:17). You see, only God's words are alive and active. My words to you in this book may bring hope to your heart, but they aren't living words. God's words, on the other hand, are "spirit words" and actually bring life to your spirit. Proverbs 4:20-23 (NLT) say:

> My child, pay attention to what I say. Listen carefully to my words. Don't lose sight of them. Let them penetrate

deep into your heart, for ***they bring life to those who find them, and healing to their whole body.*** Guard your heart above all else, for it determines the course of your life (emphasis mine).

What we plant in our hearts matters because it grows. Cognitive neuroscientist Dr. Caroline Leaf states that it takes your brain 21 days to tear down old thought patterns and another 21 days to establish new thought patterns. That's essentially what I did, though I had not read her research at the time. I took about a month to work through the negative emotional baggage I had accumulated, and then I took another month, my 30-day healing dare, to build positive statements about my health.

In Dr. Leaf's book *Switch On Your Brain: The Key to Peak Happiness, Thinking, and Health*, she states:

> Thoughts are real, physical things that occupy mental real estate.

Moment by moment, every day, you are changing the structure of your brain through your thinking. When we hope, it is an activity of the mind that changes the structure of our brain in a positive and normal direction.

Positive thinking is a Biblical principle, by the way. The Word reversed the negative constructs in my mind and started to build normal images of health. Every day during those weeks of summer turning to fall, I meditated on healing scriptures— the promises of God. I became convinced that this illness wasn't God's will and this was not how He made me. John 10:10 says, "The thief comes only to steal and kill and destroy; I have come that they may have life, and have it to the full." Like I said, I had to face the facts that I saw in the physical realm but receive my Truth from the Bible.

For me, it took 30 days to paint a new picture of health in my heart. For you, it may only take three days or even three minutes! If it's a chronic issue you've dealt with a long time, it may take three months or more before your heart is fully convinced. Just stay committed to the process, and guard your heart.

Finally, one night in my room, toward the end of that 30 days, I got it. I had planted God's living Word in my heart, and it had brought healing to my mind. I could imagine myself well! It felt like my spirit started jumping up and down with joy, like a child who has just been given the *entire* toy store for Christmas! Something inside of me did a huge 180-degree turn, and I could picture myself healthy. I could see it! My head knowledge about healing had finally become heart knowledge, and I knew that it was finished, just like Jesus said as He hung on the cross (John 19:30).

Tears streamed down my face as I worshipped God for what He had already given me! Health was mine! It was a free gift, just like salvation is a free gift. I was finally plugged into the Power Source, and surges of joy and life flowed through me. I told Jason what was going on, and we agreed to go to church the next day and ask the elders to pray with me for my healing.

That Sunday morning, I went to the altar and asked for the prayer of agreement, knowing that it was my day to receive my healing. God's power hit me so strongly, I began to weep. I knew in my heart this illness was defeated! The elders anointed me with oil as a symbol of God's presence touching me. I marked that spot as the moment I reached up and said, "Yes, God, I receive Your free gift of health in my body. So be it to me according to Your Word."

FAITH IS MY EVIDENCE

I wrote down that date and time in my bible, and I stood on that moment as evidence that I was healed. But guess what!

My body didn't appear to change at all. (Did I just hear a sigh of disappointment?) When we walked away from the altar at church, nothing had changed in the physical realm yet, but in the spiritual realm I had been healed. My body looked and felt the same, as I got into the car to go home, but that didn't matter. I had a new picture of myself. I KNEW I was healed that moment. It was finished. God's Word was MY TRUTH, despite what the facts said externally.

Jesus said in Mark 11:24 (KJV), "Therefore I say unto you, What things soever ye desire, when ye pray, believe that ye receive them, and *ye shall have them.*" And Hebrews 11:1 (KJV) says, "Now faith is the *substance* of things hoped for, the *evidence* of things not seen" (emphasis mine).

In other words, you don't have to see the answer in the physical realm before you start thanking God for it. The faith you have inside is all the evidence you need that whatever you've asked for is already yours.

Notice it says that when you pray in faith, it *is* done, and you *shall* have it. Sometimes there is a short period between the moment of faith when you pray and the moment when what you are believing for shows up in the natural. There can be a period between the "Amen" and "There it is!" That's when you have to fight the fight of staying in agreement with God's Word. If you start agreeing with the symptoms of sickness again, you have come out of agreement with God.

I had to be careful about what I said and what I was thinking after we prayed that day. I wrote down the date of our prayer for healing and reminded myself, "That's when my healing took place in the spirit, even though my body has not yet reacted to that Truth."

My dad had said that day in church, "Faith is the currency of heaven, and you can use it to get anything you need that is within God's will for your life." That really stuck with me. You and I wouldn't expect to walk out of a department store with a cart full of clothes without paying for them. Yet oftentimes we expect to walk into God's presence and magically receive healing without having faith. There legally has to be a "transaction" between you and God for Him to be able to give you what you are asking for. We can't please God or receive from God without faith!

Hebrews 10:38 says, "But my righteous one will live by faith. And I take no pleasure in the one who shrinks back." Did you know it gives God pleasure to give you good things? But when we don't "live by faith," God can't give anything good to us, and, therefore, we deny Him the pleasure of giving to us.

God's pleasure in giving to us is like a parent who gets excited to buy an amazing Christmas present for their child. If you're like me, you love finding that special gift for your child! You imagine their pleasure and reaction. But what if my child woke up Christmas morning and said, "Mom, I don't believe you bought me any Christmas presents. I don't believe you're a good mom, so I'm not coming out of my room this Christmas morning. I'm going to stay here and sulk while I play with my old, broken toys." That would be hurtful to me as a parent, and would be no fun for my child, either.

The opposite of that joyless attitude is exemplified in a child who bounces out of bed, and squeals with delight before ever seeing the Christmas tree surrounded by presents, because they fully expect you bought them something good. It makes you feel like a good parent and gives you delight to see the pure joy and expectation in your child's eyes.

It makes God happy to see you well, happy, secure, and at peace. But all those good things come by faith.

Again, what is faith? It is firm, unshakable belief in God. It's a "whatever-He-said-is-true" attitude. It is being fully convinced that God has the power to do what He's promised.

How do we get faith? *We get faith by hearing the Word of God.* As we hear scripture after scripture, Truth after Truth, a fortress is built in our minds that can withstand every trick of the enemy. Negative, fearful thoughts start to bounce right off, like arrows bounce off a stone wall.

My dad has created so many good illustrations for this principle of faith, I'm going to steal one here. (Thanks, Dad, haha!) He puts it this way: Let's say someone wrote you a check for $50,000 dollars. The person who gave you that check is a billionaire, so you are fully convinced, without a shadow of doubt, they are good for the money. Your name is written on the check, and their signature is on there, too, along with all those zeros. Now, would you get excited? Would you jump up and down? Would you immediately think about what you would spend it on? I definitely would!

But wait, do you *actually* have $50,000 in U.S. currency in your hand? Not yet. That check is a promissory note, which means you've been promised $50,000. But that check is the evidence of the $50,000 you have received. The only way you won't get that money is if you don't believe it's real and thus never go to the bank to cash the check!

If you know you have the money, you'll start acting $50,000 richer. You'll go ahead and plan how to spend it.

You have a promise from God that states, "And the prayer offered in faith will make the sick person well; the Lord will raise them up" (James 5:15a). If you believe the promise, you will start acting like it's already yours. You'll start imagining what you'll do when you feel great. You'll start seeing yourself healthy. But if you don't believe the promise, you will never take action on it.

The Bible is God's promissory note. It tells you what He's already given you. The only way you won't receive what He's promised is if you don't believe it and take action! God told you and me the Truth when He promised we could live in health. He gave us a book full of "checks" or promises. We just need to start acting like good health already belongs to us!

That's exactly what I did for the two weeks after praying the prayer of agreement, with amazing results.

CHAPTER TWO

RADICALLY HEALED

"He jumped to his feet and began to walk. Then he went with them into the temple courts, walking and jumping, and praising God. When all the people saw him walking and praising God, they recognized him as the same man who used to sit begging at the temple gate called Beautiful, and they were filled with wonder and amazement at what had happened to him."

Acts 3:8-10 (NIV)

Two weeks after receiving prayer, nothing had changed physically in my body that I could tell. Still, I kept thanking God that I had *already* been healed when I prayed, and ***I knew that I knew it was only a matter of time before my body reflected my belief.***

Praise and worship became key during this time of "resting in the waiting." I would put on meditative music and just tell God how happy I was to be healed. I thanked Him for healing me. I worshipped Him. A peace and trust was constantly in my heart over this issue. I meditated on the solution, not the struggle.

To me, it was like this: the Judge over all the universe had already made a ruling in my favor. He had ruled that I was "healed." Now, just because I couldn't see the effects of that ruling yet didn't mean it wasn't true. I still believed the Judge's words. It applied to me and my body.

The matter of my health was settled in the courts of heaven and in the realm of my heart.
Case dismissed.

SEPTEMBER 28, 2010

One night, I went to bed in a lot of muscular pain. I did my usual bedtime routine, brushed my teeth, said my scriptures, but then I did something I normally didn't do. I absentmindedly weighed myself. Then I crawled into bed.

I did not stir that night. In fact, I'm pretty sure it was the best sleep of my life!

The next morning, I groggily sat up in bed to the sound of my alarm. I groaned. My abs felt a little bit like I had worked out too much the day before. I laid back down and said to Jason, "What did I do yesterday that would have made my abs sore?" Jason looked over at me with only one eye open, then he looked down at my stomach. A look of shock spread across his sleepy face.

"Amy, look at your body!"

I looked down and touched my stomach. *For the first time in nine years, my abdomen was flat and soft.*

The hard place that had protruded for so long was totally gone! I gasped and stood up out of bed, walking on trembling legs. Excitement coursed through my veins. I bent over and easily touched my toes. No stiffness.

I pulled up my shirt and noticed that my belly button, which had been an "outie" for nine years, was an "innie" once again.

I ran to the mirror in shock. I looked so much smaller and thinner that I pinched myself just in case I was dreaming.

I decided to weigh and measure myself. The only reason I knew my waist measurements was because I had just been fitted for a bridesmaid's dress. And yes, the seamstress's comment that day had been, "Are you pregnant?"

I stepped onto the scale. I read it again. Three times.

OVERNIGHT, I HAD LOST 13 POUNDS!

I grabbed a measuring tape and put it around my waist. Before, my bust and waist measurement had been identical. Now there was a nine-inch difference.

I HAD LOST NINE INCHES FROM MY WAIST!

By this time the shock had given way to tears of thankfulness. Jason felt my spine. The vertebra weren't sticking out anymore. The curve in my lower spine was there, and for the first time in years, I felt limber and loose.

I was almost numb with a rush of emotions: joy, shock, happiness, and wonder!

God had literally done surgery on my body while I slept. The slight soreness I felt was probably from my organs moving back into place (much like a pregnant woman's after giving birth) and from my abdominal muscles that had been "deactivated" for nine years suddenly having to do the job of holding up my rib cage. That tumor wasn't there anymore!

I took a picture (below) and texted it to my mom. This is the first picture I took of my healing, wearing a shirt I would have never worn by itself before my healing.

THE FIRST PICTURE OF MY NEW BODY, ON THE MORNING OF MY MIRACLE

I got a call from Mom two minutes later, and after hearing me explain for a few seconds, she said, "I'm coming right over!" She rushed to our house. When she walked in to see me standing there, with a waistline that looked totally proportionate, she started crying. The first thing she did was come hug me close. Before, when she would hug me, she said it felt like hugging a pregnant lady. My belly would literally get in the way. But now she could hold me tight.

THE DIFFERENCE OF 8 HOURS!

BEFORE AND AFTER:
13 POUNDS AND 9 INCHES GONE!

She asked the rest of the family to all meet up at their house later that day. As I walked into the foyer, my brothers and sisters got teary-eyed when they saw me. We all shared hugs and smiles.

The next weekend, many of the people in my church saw me and were whispering amongst themselves, "What happened to her body? Look at her waist!" I wasn't quite ready to share my story until I had my family doctor confirm what I already knew.

A week later, I went to my doctor who had seen me a few times before, and she was shocked as well. She felt my stomach and back, asking what had happened. Poking around, she kept asking, "Does this hurt?" "No!" I would reply, "God healed me!" She finally acknowledged, "Well, *whoever* did this, looks like they did you a big favor!" I thought to myself, *Yes HE did!*

I had x-rays done, and the difference is astounding. In the "after" x-ray, you can see that the curve in my spine is normal.

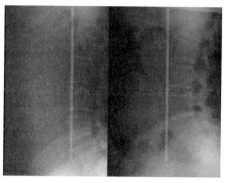

BEFORE
Spine is straight,
intestines are displaced,
mass in abdomen.

AFTER
Spine is curved,
intestines are in place,
mass is gone.

I added a straight line to each x-ray so you can compare the curvature. But more than the look of my spine shape, the way it felt was immensely different than before. Every muscle felt so loose now, with no pain!

I was actually very clumsy those first few weeks due to lack of muscle tone in my abdomen, because those muscles had not been used properly for years. I had no core strength. In fact, I had a fall and got a slightly bruised rib thanks to not having the core strength to properly break my fall. (Personal trainers will tell you that the best way to avoid injury is to work on your core muscle strength!) I had to slowly build up muscle tone.

Despite my clumsiness, I immediately started enjoying my brand-new body. I felt like I was doing so many things for the very first time! Everything was new. I could move and stretch in ways I couldn't before. My curves were back. I could stand for hours, as I often do in my role as worship leader at my church. I was and still am completely pain free!

I had the joy of sharing my story at my church, during which everyone who had known me over the years wept and wept. No one could deny that I had encountered the supernatural power of God!

CHILDREN OF MY FAITH

You remember my "Hannah's prayer"? One year after my healing, on our second anniversary, we prayed for children—a girl with curly brown hair and light eyes, and a little boy who looked like Jason. (I don't know why we went ahead and prayed for our first **two** children, but we did, haha!) We also prayed that our firstborn would be very wise and strong, with prophetic insight.

I had fearful thoughts try to come, as all women do, wondering if I could get pregnant. *What if something still isn't normal in there? What if I'm not totally healed? What if I can't have a good delivery?* The enemy whispered lies throughout that month. "Shut up, satan!" I would say each time those thoughts would come.

One morning, about a month after we prayed, I secretly took a pregnancy test just after arriving at church for meetings. I had no symptoms of pregnancy, except I could not get enough Italian food! That's all I had wanted for weeks. Jason was already in our first meeting, but I snuck away for a moment to take the test.

When those two pink lines showed up on that test, I did a double take. It was positive! Tears of joy sprang to my eyes, and I kept saying over and over again, "We have a baby!" I rushed to the meeting room hoping to catch Jason before the speaker started, but alas, it was too late.

I composed myself and tried to look normal, all the while barely containing my excitement. I probably had a ridiculous smile on my face the entire time as the speaker talked about this form and that procedure... blah, blah, blah. I didn't hear a word, haha! Oh, the torture of having to wait! As soon as the meeting dismissed, I grabbed Jason's hand and rushed him into my office.

As soon as the door closed, he said, "You're pregnant, aren't you?!"

"How did you know?" I gasped.

"We prayed, didn't we?" he replied with a laugh and a hug.

After a pain-free pregnancy, during which my back and hips *never* hurt, I gave birth to our beautiful daughter. My body worked perfectly with no complications, and it was a wonderful experience. In fact, I had no interventions or medications of any kind during the delivery. The moment I looked into the wide eyes of that little 6-pound, 8-ounce baby girl, I realized this was the completion of my journey of faith.

We decided to name her Journey Taylor because of the journey of faith it took to get her. Today she is an incredibly wise, smart, strong little girl with curly brown hair and light blue eyes. She looks pretty much like a mini me. She was talking in full paragraphs and easily carrying on conversations with adults by the time she was a year old; and one of her first phrases was "Praise Jesus!" She is such a joy, and we constantly get compliments on how smart she is.

Then 19 months later, God blessed us with our second miracle, our son, Dawson James, who looks just like his daddy. He is so snuggly, strong, handsome, and charismatic. I call him my little spark of joy, because he lights up the room and you can hear him coming from a mile away! We are enjoying his amazing personality and boundless physical energy.

Four years later, we prayed for another sweet blessing to be added to our family, and nine months later we had Revere Everett. With blonde hair, blue eyes, and the most fetching smile you've ever seen, he is definitely my calm, calculated, methodical child.

I absolutely love being a mommy! I am living in the dreams of my younger self, and I am so grateful.

Based on the pain I was in before my healing, I truly believe I would not have been able to carry a baby and have normal pregnancies and deliveries—but my Father is greater!

I want to share a few more amazing stories of people who were radically healed. I want you to understand that there is hope for ANY issue you're facing. When I sat through the "Live Whole" teaching series at my church during my 30-day challenge, I heard story after story of supernatural miracles. Those stories really sparked my hope. I want you to know that same hope. Let me share some other impossible situations that God totally changed around!

A LIFELONG ASTHMATIC

The Sunday I shared my story of healing at my home church, Sarah was touched. She had struggled with chronic asthma since she was a toddler. But her life was about to change forever. Here's her amazing story, in her own words:

When I was very young, I began experiencing asthma symptoms. I remember how scared I was each time I had an attack. The feeling of my airways constricting and the struggle to breathe is still a vivid memory. So many times, my mum would have to take me to the emergency room because my inhalers were not helping. I would sit in the car as she drove, wheezing, and my fingertips would start to tingle because my body was not getting enough oxygen to my extremities. I lost count of the amount of hospital trips we did over the years growing up. My mum actually worked night shift in the emergency room of a hospital, so there were times when she took me to work with her because I frequently had nighttime asthma attacks.

Doctors always said, "Well, children grow out of it," but as I got older, I didn't. Then it went from, "She'll grow out of it," to "She'll be fine and can live a normal life, as long as she is compliant and sticks with her medication regimen." Somewhere along the line, I just accepted what they said. I learned to take my inhalers; and when it was flaring up, I'd take Prednisone, a nasty steroid. It became a part of my life. I slept with an inhaler under my pillow, and carried one in my purse at all times.

My mum had great faith in God. When my older brother was diagnosed with cancer, she refused to accept the diagnosis. She called her pastor and they prayed. That was a good 20 years ago now. He was indeed healed of cancer.

She would also pray for me and have pastors pray for me for healing from asthma. But I never went a day without using my inhalers. It wasn't that I didn't think God could heal me. I'd seen evidence that miracles can happen. So to be honest, I was happy other people received healing, and continued to live my life. I'd been taking those same rescue inhalers and corticosteroids for almost 30 years! Indeed, the doctors were right: asthma is not a death sentence if you stick to their medication regimen.

But why put up with something if you can live whole?

My husband, Stephen, and I have been attending Faith Life Church in Ohio for the past year. In October, during a Sunday service, a lady named Amy got up and gave her testimony of how God healed her. As Amy began to share how she had been to many doctors in hopes of an answer, she said something that really hit me. She said doctors had told her that they didn't know why her body was the way it was, but that it was her "normal." So she accepted it.

I immediately realized that I, too, had chosen to accept what the facts were, and what the doctors said. I realized that in doing so I had trusted their words over THE Word, God's Word, the Bible.

I began to cry uncontrollably, I was shaking, and I just knew that I had been missing out on my healing all those years because of that. As she continued to share, I sat crying. But in that time, I just knew that God had healed me.

The next morning I woke up, and I didn't take any inhalers. As I began going about my day and getting ready for a day at the zoo with my boys, I realized I didn't take any medication like I usually do. I felt fear and anxiety building, and then I felt my airways begin to constrict. So what happened? Was I not really healed?

I had two things I could do: give in to that fear and take the inhaler, or speak to that fear. I chose to speak to it! I grabbed my Bible and some scrap pieces of paper, and I wrote down Bible verses on healing. As I wrote, I said them out loud. Then I went back to making lunch for the boys and kept speaking those words over my body. Within minutes, all airway tightness in my chest was alleviated, and I was able to breathe with no wheezing!

For a moment that morning as I began to feel tightness in my chest, I confess, I questioned my healing. But that thought was fleeting. As I opened my Bible, I began to read this scripture in Matthew 9:22:

Jesus turned and saw her.

"Take heart, daughter," he said, "your faith has healed you." And the woman was healed from that moment."

That scripture cemented in my mind what I knew to be true. God had indeed healed me as I sat in church listening to Amy's testimony. I continue to carry those scrap pieces of paper with the scriptures written on them. In fact, I keep them in a pocket in my purse...the same pocket I used to carry my inhaler in! I pull them out and speak those words over my body. I don't look at the facts anymore; I listen to THE Truth! I am healed!

Sarah went from taking inhalers every day of her life to never needing one again! How? When I said that I had accepted my health problem as my "normal" and this was "just the way I was," she realized that's what she had done. She decided enough was enough. She was ready for a new way of life—a life of freedom! The tears continued to flow as she stepped forward at the end of the service and asked me to pray with her for her healing. "I know it's already done! I am healed!" she said as she left the front of the church.

When that asthma attack tried to come on the next day, she shut out the voice of fear and turned on the voice of faith! She took her stand, and she felt that God was telling her to let go of the things that reminded her of the sickness, so she even threw away her medications. The symptoms left, and she has been breathing normally since that day, healed of lifelong asthma!

A CREATIVE MIRACLE

I received this message soon after sharing about my healing. It's from my friend Cortney, whom I have known all my life. She wrote:

Since I was about 12 years old, we noticed my left leg was much shorter than my right leg, and it caused a lot of discomfort in my back and my leg. I just assumed I was made that way intentionally.

So years passed and I got married and then had two babies, and it was extremely hard on my back to have the weight of the baby and the off-centeredness of my left leg. It caused a lot of pain.

After Amy Freudiger gave her testimony about how she stopped settling for imperfection and started telling her body to line up, I was intrigued. And since my pastor was teaching a healing series, I decided it was time to change my mind-set. I started telling my leg to even out and be whole...and in the beginning of February, I went up for the prayer of agreement with the elders. That night I felt a "release" in my spirit.

Five days later, I was getting ready for bed and I noticed soreness in my lower back, almost like the feeling of working out really hard. I didn't really read into it.

That night I got in the shower, and all of a sudden it hit me—I wasn't leaning while I stood! I was standing on both legs evenly! I started crying and told my husband, Clint, that it was whole, and it was now how God intended it to be!

I am pregnant with my third baby, and this pregnancy has just been amazing! No back pain and no more awkward standing positions! PRAISE GOD!!!

Cortney had another encounter with the power of God that was even more dramatic. One day she, along with her aunt, discovered her little cousin floating lifelessly at the bottom of a backyard pool. He was blue and was not breathing. No one knew how long he had been down there, but he showed no signs of life.

Instead of freaking out, Cortney knew they had authority over the spirit of death, so she said, "Let's not call 9-1-1; let's speak to him in the name of Jesus!" So Cortney and her aunt began commanding the child to wake up, in the name of Jesus. Moments later, he awoke, coughed a bunch of water out of his lungs, and started breathing again.

It might have been too late by the time an ambulance came. Sometimes we have mere seconds to react in either faith or fear. Life and death hang in the balance! Thank God that Cortney and her aunt knew God's will for that situation.

PLANNING HER OWN FUNERAL

Lisa, a beautiful blond-haired lady with a warm smile, had just received impossible news: she needed to get her affairs in order because doctors couldn't do anything else for her. She found herself planning her own funeral. Hope was lost, and her doctors told her there was nothing else to do but wait to die.

You see, she was suffering from a life-threatening connective tissue disease, a kind of autoimmune disorder in which her body was literally attacking itself. This sweet wife and mother, who had once been an energetic lady, was completely void of life and strength now. She was also bleeding internally, and doctors couldn't do anything to help. Sounds like another woman I've read about.

Mark 5:25-28 tell us this story:

> And a woman was there who had been subject to bleeding for twelve years. She had suffered a great deal under the care of many doctors and had spent all she had, yet instead of getting better

she grew worse. When she heard about Jesus, she came up behind him in the crowd and touched his cloak, because she thought, "If I just touch his clothes, I will be healed."

Just like Lisa, this woman with the bleeding issue had no hope of getting well. Perhaps she was shocked when she heard of all that Jesus had done in the villages, healing leprosy and blindness, and even raising people from the dead. But she knew that she had to see this man who was curing things the doctors said were incurable. A glimmer of hope was sparked in her heart.

Lisa and her husband heard about my church and that there was something different about the people who went there— they received answers from God for their problems! Lisa decided to give it a try. On their first visit, they received a teaching series on the Kingdom of God, so she popped it in one day as she lay listless on the couch. She was shocked when she heard that it wasn't

God's will that she be sick! At first, she was offended, even angry, that the pastor was saying her condition wasn't "part of God's plan," as some say. But she heard scripture after scripture to back up this claim.

And so they kept going back to our church each weekend, and Lisa decided to look further into this healing thing herself. She began studying God's Word and listening to more teachings. She heard my story, as well as the "Live Whole" series I had listened to around the time I was healed.

And just like the woman in the Bible, Lisa decided to come to Jesus, putting her faith in Him. One Sunday in a church service, God spoke through the pastor (my father) to say that someone was being healed of hemorrhaging. Lisa and her husband looked at each other, eyes wide, and Lisa whispered, "That's me!" In that moment, her bleeding stopped! The doctors confirmed this fact the next week.

That's what happened to the woman in

the Bible, too! "Immediately her bleeding stopped and she felt in her body that she was freed from her suffering" (Mark 5:29).

Now, Jesus says something that sounds strange for God-in-the-flesh to ask:

> At once Jesus realized that power had gone out from him. He turned around in the crowd and asked, "Who touched my clothes?"
>
> "You see the people crowding against you," his disciples answered, "and yet you can ask, 'Who touched me?'" But Jesus kept looking around to see who had done it (Mark 5:30-32).

If Jesus, God's Son, had just arbitrarily decided, "Yes, I think I will heal this woman today," wouldn't He have known who it was who touched Him? So if Jesus didn't make an arbitrary decision to finally free this woman from her suffering, why was she healed when she touched Jesus's coat? Jesus answers that question:

Then the woman, knowing what had happened to her, came and fell at his feet and, trembling with fear, told him the whole truth. He said to her, "Daughter, your faith has healed you. Go in peace and be freed from your suffering" (Mark 5:33-34).

My point is it was her faith that drew the power of God to her like a magnet! As my father says, people tend to think that if Jesus was in their bedroom, surely He could fix all their problems. After all, isn't Jesus awesome in His power?! If only He would have pity on their horrible circumstance and heal them. But that attitude of "waiting on God to do something" is why many Christians are never healed. They think if they cry and beg and fast and whine long enough, God will finally hear them.

These people are awaiting a decision from God to heal them. But do you know what?

God already decided to heal them!

That's why He sent Jesus to "carry our infirmities." If "by His stripes [the whipping Jesus took on His back before being crucified] you WERE healed" then you ARE healed! (See Isaiah 53:5 and 1 Peter 2:24.) God already decided to heal them and is now waiting on *them* to simply take the gift He already gave them. How does one receive their healing then?

Firm, unshakable belief (faith) in God's promise is what draws the power of God to fulfill that promise. Jesus told the woman with the issue of blood that her faith had made her whole.

Because God already chose to bring healing to humanity through Jesus, this woman's faith in that fact was what healed her. God doesn't change, so the same is true for you and for me.

And the same was true for Lisa, who was not only healed from her hemorrhaging, but also from the connective tissue disease! She received back her full strength! She went from planning her own funeral to making a full recovery, astounding her doctors, and taking back her life with renewed purpose and vigor. She now spends her time praying for people to be set free, and she tells everyone the good news: God's will is that we live in health!

PARALYSIS GONE

When my parents and I traveled to the Philippines, we met a man who was carried to the conference meeting by his friends. He had suffered a stroke and was paralyzed on his right side. He was in so much pain he could not move, and his friends were all trying to figure out how to support his family since he could not work. At the end of the service, he was carried down front for prayer. Suddenly, the power of God hit him, and he jumped up, waving his arms. He then started running around the room praising God, and all of his friends joined him! I'll never forget seeing a paralyzed man walk!

That reminds me of the story in Luke 5:18-26. Jesus had reached rock star status in his city because of all the healings taking place. One day some men heard of where Jesus was teaching, and they were determined to get their paralyzed friend there. Only, when they got there, all the front row seats were taken. So they got the crazy idea to lower their friend through the roof! Sure enough, the paralytic made his grand entrance, being lowered down on his mat. That got everyone's attention. The story gets better:

> When Jesus saw their faith, he said, "Friend, your sins are forgiven."
>
> The Pharisees and the teachers of the law began thinking to themselves, "Who is this fellow who speaks blasphemy? Who can forgive sins but God alone?"
>
> Jesus knew what they were thinking and asked, "Why are you thinking these things in your hearts? Which is easier:

to say, 'Your sins are forgiven,' or to say, 'Get up and walk'? But I want you to know that the Son of Man has authority on earth to forgive sins."

So he said to the paralyzed man, "I tell you, get up, take your mat and go home." Immediately he stood up in front of them, took what he had been lying on and went home praising God. Everyone was amazed and gave praise to God. They were filled with awe and said, "We have seen remarkable things today."

DEAF EAR OPENS

At a class where I told my story of healing, I met a lady named Christine who had been gradually losing her hearing for 42 years, and she was at only 50% hearing. The doctor told her she would eventually be 100% deaf. In fact, deafness ran in her family. She wore hearing aids, and she was tired of it, so when she heard my story, she made a decision. Christine came up for prayer at the end of this class and said, "I'm done with this! I want my hearing back. I'm ready!"

She was brand new to our church, having been raised Catholic. She had never before heard that Jesus was still doing miracles today, and that was all she needed. She grabbed hold of that one promise. She didn't need 20 years of theology lessons— she had innocent, childlike faith in that moment to receive from her Daddy God.

My mother and I prayed for her and she said, "I feel heat! I'm tingling!" Her feet got so hot she started dancing up and down, laughing! Then her ears opened up, and she started screaming, "I can hear!" She started running around the room, screaming and laughing. Her hearing was at 100%! She took those hearing aids out and said, "I'm throwing these things in the trash!" And she's never had another hearing issue.

The same Jesus who healed me, who healed my friends, and who healed the sick in the Bible is the same Jesus who is extending the gift of healing to you. He doesn't play favorites. He offers His healing power to all who call on His name.

CHAPTER THREE

FIVE STEPS
TO YOUR
MIRACLE

*"...they shall lay hands on the sick, and
they shall recover."*

Mark 16:18b (KJV)

You may be thinking, *Well, isn't that nice. She had a miracle. But what about my problems? Why hasn't God done anything about them?*

I want to challenge you that what God does for one, He promised He will do for all. Let me share the five most important steps that God showed me to take in receiving my healing.

1. RECLAIM YOUR IDENTITY.

Everyone identifies themselves as something. Perhaps labels such as "Sick," "Unworthy," "Angry," "Broken," "Stupid," "Ugly," "Broke," or "Victim" have become your identity. It's time to ditch that identity crisis!

When I started praying about healing, God first showed me the false identities I had assumed. He showed me that I could not begin to see myself healed because my identity was all wrong. I was calling myself by the wrong names. Let me elaborate on this principle a bit more, because it was my starting point.

Fill in the blank: "Hello, my name is _____, and I am _____."

Whether or not we realize it, we make statements about our identities every day. "**I am scared** to death of that." "I almost had a **heart attack** when...." "**I am sick** of this." "**I am** tired." "**I can't** take it anymore!" "The doctor says **my** headaches are here to stay." *These are all statements of ownership or identity.* The greatest discovery God led me to during my journey of faith was the restoration of my identity.

Let me share with you the one truth that made all the difference for me: *"Healed" is <u>who</u> I am—it's not something I'm trying to obtain.*

Healed is *who* I am. It's a statement of ownership and identity. When I was sick, I was suffering from an identity crisis due to self-hatred, and it was blocking my healing. You see, you and I were born into royalty, in God's house, but through the fall of man caused by Adam and Eve, we contracted amnesia. We forgot who we really were created to be.

We are heirs to a Kingdom so vast, it cannot be measured, and it's time to ditch the identity crisis to stand in that Truth. We are co-heirs with Christ (Romans 8:17). ***But if we forget who we are, we forget that to which we have access.*** Our Father OWNS the universe, but we live so far below our potential as His kids! That's why we have to constantly look in the mirror God gave us—His Words to us in the Bible. God will show who we are through the Bible, but just one look is not enough.

James 1:23-25 say it like this:

> Anyone who listens to the word but does not do what it says is like

someone who looks at his face in a mirror and, after looking at himself, goes away and immediately forgets what he looks like. But whoever looks intently into the perfect law that gives freedom, and continues in it—not forgetting what they have heard but doing it—they will be blessed in what they do.

If the Bible says *I am* healed (1 Peter 2:24), that is a statement about my identity. Healed is not just what I am... healed is WHO I am. All during my struggle, I was a child of God with citizenship in His Kingdom, but I was allowing an evil presence to attack my body and "live in my territory." A spirit of infirmity was attacking the image of God in me. I internalized that sickness and made it part of *who I was.* It was corrupting my true identity as the Healer's child. It was outside of my spiritual DNA.

Kenneth Copeland once said, "I have

to choose to lean to my spiritual DNA, rather than to my natural DNA." My spiritual DNA is the very same as God's because I was made in His image. That doesn't mean I am God, just like my daughter is not me. But she sure looks like me! Therefore, if something comes into my body that doesn't match that god-like DNA code, it is not from God. (Your covenant is spelled out in Deuteronomy 28 and through the actions of Jesus.)

Sickness is an illegal violation of my covenant rights, according to the laws of God, and satan has no right to trespass on my property. I was translated (my citizenship moved) out of the kingdom of darkness, and I became born again as a different person—a brand-new version of me (Colossians 1:13).

I am a child of the light. God changed my name when I came into His family. When I gave my life to Him, essentially becoming His bride, He gave me His name! When I became bound to Him, I separated myself from darkness. That darkness includes sickness. It cannot remain in the light unless I dim that light and allow darkness in.

A spiritual identity crisis is often an indication that emotional healing needs to take place. Emotional healing brings freedom, and it usually happens before or in tandem with physical healing. Deep emotional wounds can keep you from receiving, because the enemy can use that particular area in the soul realm to break your agreement with God. You can receive emotional healing from the Lord, but first you have to release the control of those wounds to Him.

What if your hands were full of rocks, and a friend was trying to hand you a gift? You would have to drop the rocks before you could take the beautifully wrapped gift. In the same way, there are things we must let go of before we can receive anything from God. "Rocks" such as unforgiveness, bitterness, unworthiness, or strife are like rock walls that block God's blessings. Unforgiveness toward ourselves or others is an especially huge roadblock to receiving anything from God. Confess it, and then if possible, go to the person you are offended with to make it right. Soul-realm maladies are at the root of all kinds of sickness, so let them go and stop allowing them to contaminate your DNA. Realize those are foreign entities trying to twist the character of God in you.

Healing isn't just about the physical body. You are three parts: spirit, soul, and body. It says in 3 John 2 (KJV):

> Beloved, I wish above all things that thou mayest prosper and be in health, even as thy soul prospereth.

Wholeness in the body is also about wholeness in the emotional and spiritual parts of us too. In fact, many times, emotional disorders, trauma, and stress can be at the root of physical problems.

When I was seeking God for healing, I began to realize that I had some emotional identity thieves working against me. I had some people to forgive, I had some emotional patterns to break, I had some attitudes to confront, and I had some baggage to let go of. I didn't even realize how heavy the hurts and doubts had grown until God showed me how they were controlling my thoughts and reactions to situations. They were affecting my relationships.

Forgiving others is so key, but I also had to forgive myself. I had to forgive myself for "failure to perform perfectly." I had believed the lie that my value was based on my performance. I was often extremely stressed because I was constantly working to measure up, to be good, to be adequate, to be "enough." I would do anything for anybody and had an issue saying "No."

Performance-based value has adverse affects on our health because it results in stress. Did you know that 77% of people in the United States regularly experience stress related symptoms? The annual costs to employers for stress-related health care and missed work is around $300 billion (Statistic Brain Research Institute, American Institute of Stress, N.Y., October 17, 2015). Performance-based value will land you in the E.R., the psychiatric ward, or even an early grave due to stress! It will give you a nervous breakdown. It will steal your joy because you can never be "good enough."

In myself, I'm not enough. I can't be perfect. I had to learn that, acknowledge it, and be okay with it. The Truth is, "For all have sinned and *fall short* of the glory of God..." (Romans 3:23, emphasis mine).

Then I discovered that with Jesus, *I am more than enough*!

Romans 8:37 says, "No, in all these things we are more than conquerors through him who loved us."

Philippians 4:13 (NLT) says, "For I can do everything *through Christ*, who gives me strength" (emphasis mine).

Romans 8:26a (NLT) says, "And the Holy Spirit helps us in our weakness." That was a discovery that was a long time in coming, and it's one that has continued to revolutionize my life. Say this with me, "Through God's grace, I am enough!"

Because I am a peacemaker, I also had to stop basing my happiness and peace on others' happiness. I realized I cannot make everyone happy. It's humanly impossible. If there are people I care about who are not happy, the best thing I can do is pray for them, not become unhappy myself. Empathy can quickly become "taking up someone else's offense."

Maybe the identity thieves of control, rejection, abandonment, or pride are the soul sicknesses operating against you. It's time to break free! *God has given you power to deal with the causes and find a new source of peace in Him.*

The traditional Jewish greeting *Shalom*

means *nothing missing, nothing broken.* That's you when you dwell in Christ! Being in the presence of Love, Himself is like having a healing balm poured over your wounds and broken places. Only Jesus can heal those things.

Through my journey to wholeness, I had to ask the Holy Spirit to show me the lies I had believed about myself. Being married to a wonderful man of God also helped reveal some of the insecurities I clung to. Marriage generally has a way of uncovering issues we didn't know we had, haha! It helped reveal the voices of unworthiness, control, and performance that I had listened to.

When Jason echoed the voice of Father God to me, speaking beauty, worth, and loveliness into my soul, he was reinforcing what the Father was saying about me. At first, my mind rejected many of the things Jason said, because I didn't believe them. But over time, God taught me I had to learn to receive compliments.

It's important to surround yourself with people who will encourage your faith, whether they are your spouse, parents, family members, or friends. Plus, remember that you have The Most Powerful One, the Holy Spirit, speaking life to you. Listen to Him!

If you have someone in your life who is struggling with darkness, let me encourage you to reinforce the voice of God in their life simply by speaking what God says about them. Your words can set someone else free!

For all those years, the real me was living in the shadows. But when I finally took out the Word and allowed it to light me up on the inside, darkness tucked its tail and ran!

It can be a process to reclaim your identity, but don't get discouraged. Keep pressing on!

Take action: Reclaim your spiritual identity through God's Word. Let Him show you the rocks you are holding onto, and let them go by faith.

2. REPAINT YOUR PICTURE.

All right, it's time for your own 30-day healing dare! Are you ready?! If you have something wrong in your body that you have accepted as your normal—as your truth—it's time to change that picture! The only way to do that is to go to the source of Truth, the Word of God. I DARE YOU to focus every bit of your attention on the Bible, and to lend your voice to what God says instead of what every other voice says. Read it! Listen to it! Speak it! And then do it again and again!

It's time to obsess over the picture of hope, health, and healing that Jesus gave us. Shut off the other messages, take away the distractions (hello, Netflix), and remove fearful voices.

The Truth says GOD WANTS YOU WELL. If Jesus healed EVERY person who came to Him in faith, He will STILL heal

every person who comes to Him in faith.
His will does not change. He is the same
yesterday, today, and forever (Hebrews
13:8).

Our doubt, however, can get in the way of
God's will. Romans 8:6 and 12-14 (NLT) say
it this way:

> So letting your sinful nature control
> your mind leads to death. But letting
> the Spirit control your mind leads to life
> and peace. Therefore dear brothers and
> sisters, you have no obligation to do
> what your sinful nature urges you to
> do. For if you live by its dictates, you
> will die. But if through the power of
> the Spirit you put to death the deeds of
> your sinful nature, you will live. For all
> who are led by the Spirit are children
> of God.

We must not lean to our sinful earth
thinking any longer. We must lean to the

Spirit on the inside of us, calling us to walk in the power and glory and anointing of Jesus! We must not believe a physical fact—something a doctor or family member has said or how we feel today—MORE than we believe God's Truth.

We've grown up hearing about death all our lives. We cannot trust our knee-jerk reactions, emotions, or thoughts because we were trained to be professional worriers in the "valley of the shadow of death" (Psalm 23:4), as my dad says.

Think about how many medical commercials you hear on the radio and TV if you turn them on for five minutes! "If you have had chicken pox, then the shingles virus is already in you." "Do you battle such-and-such? You might need this-or-that." "You might be among the 30% of women who have this." "If you are feeling this way, you might have this disease." Let me tell you, fear never got anyone healed, so it's time to turn that junk off! Shut off the sources of fear! Silence the voice of fear! Then start replacing it with Truth.

You must bombard your mind with healthy thoughts to replace that picture of fear, pain, and sickness with the right picture of health. You must rediscover who you really are through Christ. Isaiah 53:5 gives a picture of the gift of health we were given when Jesus gave His life for us on the cross:

> But he was pierced for our transgressions, he was crushed for our iniquities; the punishment that brought us peace was upon him, and by his wounds we are healed.

The New Living Translation says it this way:

> He was pierced for our rebellion, crushed for our sins. He was beaten so we could be whole. *He was*

whipped so we could be healed (emphasis mine).

I don't know about you, but I don't want to reject or waste this gift Jesus gave me. I want to receive the wholeness and healing this verse is talking about. I don't want to let one drop of Jesus's blood go to waste because of my unbelief.

As your vision for your body changes from one of death to one of life, you also want to apply that vision to the choices you are making for your body. When you see yourself as healthy, vibrant, energetic, in shape, joyful, powerful, and in control of your decisions, you start acting like it! You start living like it!

That's where natural wisdom comes in. The phrase "diet and exercise" is one we hear a lot, but it's one that most people are not willing to pursue because they lack vision for their lives. Vision will dictate your actions concerning your health. You won't eat thousands of sugar calories if you have a vision of longevity and legacy building.

God has given wisdom to us through His Word, and *He has also placed natural principles for health in the earth.* For instance, He has created many plants with superpowers to fuel and restore the body.

He has also given wisdom to men and women—doctors, chiropractors, personal trainers, nutritionists, etc.—who can help us understand these natural healing principles of the body. They can help us enact those principles. God created the body to heal itself when given the correct environment and fuel. Any intervention a doctor does is simply to help the body heal itself, because no doctor can make a cell mend or make an organ work. But they can understand what will tell that cell to mend or that organ to work.

A physical will point people toward healthy choices. For instance, if you are 100 pounds overweight and go to a doctor for joint pain, he or she should recommend some diet changes. That's wisdom. God can use a doctor to apply His wisdom to a situation, perhaps to remove infection, to set a broken bone, or to discover root causes. In fact, if it were up to satan, there would be no such thing as good doctors.

But I want to caution you that ***this natural wisdom does not supersede spiritual Truth, nor does a diagnosis from a doctor outweigh the power of God to heal.***

The most dramatic lesson concerning changing my picture that God taught me through this whole thing was this: ***Faith looks at the "after" picture when the mirror still shows the "before."***

Until you can picture in your mind's eye what you are believing God for, until you can truly see it happening in your life, you won't be able to receive it. When I say, "Picture what you are believing God for," you should be able to see it in your mind's eye, define it, name it, and know it's possible.

When I was sick in my body, it was hard for me to get that picture of health, because doctors couldn't say what was wrong with me. Therefore, I really didn't know what to pray against except some of the symptoms I was feeling. But for some reason, when I finally saw those X-rays, I could see what was wrong: My spine wasn't curved, and there was a mass that needed to be gone. That activated my imagination to picture those things reversed and healed.

In repainting our picture of health, we need to deal with how we picture medical answers coming. We have to deal with our idolization of scientific medicine. Many of us treat doctors' words as final. We picture them as our only hope. The instant we face any pain or sickness, our first thought often is not what God says, but instead is what the pain med bottle says or what a medical website says.

In the Western world, we tend to see doctors and hospitals as *the* answer. I'm not saying science lies, but I am saying there is a Greater Power than science. The One who *created* science knows a thing or two more than what your doctor knows.

Here's the thing: God requires our full heart allegiance in order for Him to have access to our lives. ***Supernatural healing will never come if it is a Plan B in your mind.*** God cannot be Plan B. So let me ask you, where is your trust? Either everything Jesus said is true, or NOTHING He said is true. Either what He did on the Cross is enough for everything, or it is just a nice story. Ouch. That's tough to hear, but know that I say it as your friend and partner in this journey to health.

It's okay to see a great doctor who is an agent of health, but trust God as the Healer. It's okay to consider medical intervention as part of God's answer if He leads you that way, but it should never be where your confidence and trust lie. The supernatural realm of God and His Kingdom supersedes the natural realm of this earthly kingdom. It's more powerful. It is the final word, even when doctors can offer no hope of a cure.

Doctors are trained to give a diagnosis and prognosis (the likely course of a disease or ailment) based strictly on natural ability and knowledge, minus spiritual intervention, and usually based on a worst-case scenario. Take that into consideration if you put yourself under a doctor's care, and remember that their word is not above God's Word. Pray for your doctor to have wisdom and to speak words of life over you. Get a second or third opinion. Stand against any words that don't line up with the Truth.

I am certainly not against doctors, but I *am* against some all-too-common practices. For instance, I am against medicating the symptoms of things like depression and not dealing with the root causes. I am against reckless prescribing of needless drugs and surgeries without first pursuing natural remedies, such as diet and exercise. I am against the fear-based culture that exists in the medical community. I am against some of the pharmaceutical industry's business practices, such as marketing like crazy to doctors so they prescribe their drugs, causing overprescribing and higher costs to the end user. Most of all, I am against putting faith in any human being *above* putting faith in God.

Let's talk about prevention for a moment. It's our job to give our bodies the fuel and good environment to stay healthy. Oftentimes, we do the opposite—there are so many unhealthy influences in our culture! Sometimes, satan doesn't have to do anything, because we are the ones causing physical damage through our food intake, lack of liquids, and lack of exercise.

Poor diet or lack of exercise can indeed be at the root of physical problems. Don Colbert, M.D. says he believes most illnesses can be prevented and even cured with diet, healed emotions, and a healthy lifestyle. If you ask God, He will show you what is at the root of your health challenges and if there are things you need to change so your body can heal.

If you're eating sugar and white flour every day, that might be the root cause of your diabetes. If you are severely overweight, there are a host of issues to which you are opening the door. If you are only getting a few hours of sleep per night, you aren't giving your body time to recover. If you aren't eating whole, nutritious foods and instead are constantly consuming fast food, you are introducing harmful elements into your system without giving it the tools to detox.

Ask the Holy Spirit to guide you in your day-to-day decisions and to give you the power to accomplish your goals.

Ultimately, we must make the right decisions for our bodies. I often confess over myself, "I have the same self-discipline that Jesus had because I have the same Spirit on the inside of me! I can make good choices in my eating and exercise so I can run my race well!"

When we look at Jesus's daily life, we see that He was extremely self-disciplined. Guess what?! We can be too. He stayed on task with His assignment, and so can we. He did not let anything pull Him off of His mission, and neither should we. He ran His race well, and so can we. We can do it through the power of God!

As you start your 30-day healing dare, I want to say that this is not a magic formula, and it doesn't necessarily need to be as long or as short as 30 days. Do it as long as needed to repaint your picture and cause your heart to come into agreement.

Take action: Take the 30-day healing dare by turning off media that isn't faith-filled and by speaking Scriptures and declarations out loud all day long.

172

3. STAND IN YOUR AUTHORITY.

As you reclaim your identity AND change your picture through Scripture, faith builds. When faith grows, so does your boldness. You start to see that you have been given authority. Faith is always accompanied by authority. Let's talk about the "power twins" of faith and authority for a moment.

Like I said before, the definition of faith is, very simply, *full agreement with God's will.* If we can get our hearts to agree with God instead of agreeing with the sickness, symptoms, or circumstance, then God has a legal right to touch us. But that's when we must use authority to receive it. *To take authority means to confidently enforce the victory already given to us on the cross.*

Who you are in Christ (identity), plus faith in God (belief), spoken in authority (legal enforcement), equals results.

God has given us authority to speak

and bring His will here on earth as it is in heaven.

We receive healing just like we receive salvation. How do we receive salvation? We speak words of prayer when we believe. Romans 10:9 NLT) says:

> If you openly declare that Jesus is Lord and believe in your heart that God raised him from the dead, you will be saved.

So to receive healing, we must openly speak when we believe (faith). Luke 10:19 says:

> I have given you authority to trample on snakes and scorpions and to overcome all the power of the enemy; nothing will harm you.

If you are sick today, please know this: What God did for me, He will do for anyone. It was already paid for and given to you on the Cross. God is so excited for the moment when your faith takes hold of the promise! But until then, He does not have access.

Doesn't God have the legal right to do anything He wants? Yes… and no. God gave man a free will, and He cannot do what we do not want Him to do or have not given Him permission to do. God will not violate our free will.

Our faith, released through words of authority, gives God permission to invade our problem with His remedy.

You may say, "Of course I want God to heal me! Please, God, heal me!" But until your heart comes into agreement with God (faith), and you take what He ALREADY gave you on the Cross (authority), then God cannot "legally" move. He would be trespassing against what you *really* believe.

People (and satan) hear what your mouth is saying, but God hears what your heart is saying. Your heart and mouth must be in unison, saying the same thing God is saying about your circumstances. As my dad says, when the two pictures match, that's when you should pray and receive it.

People often ask me how to "get in faith" and what they should do to make themselves believe. ***Here's the thing: you can't make your heart believe anything— your heart will believe what you put into it.*** Faith grows by planting the Word of God (Romans 10:17). If you've been planting seeds of death, saying bad things about your health, then your heart will produce that and your body will go into action to bring about the things you are speaking. But if you plant good things in your heart, it will bring a good harvest.

The Bible says Jesus did good things, healing *all* who were oppressed by the devil (Acts 10:38). Start meditating on the good things Jesus did, and it will cause faith to rise. Good seeds will sprout and grow.

Unbelief is like poison in the heart. It kills the seeds before they can produce a harvest. Jesus couldn't heal many people in His hometown because they did not have faith in Him. They had known Him all His life and were too familiar with Him to believe He was the Son of God. Mark 6:5-6 (NLT) say:

> And because of their unbelief, he couldn't do any miracles among them except to place his hands on a few sick people and heal them. And he was amazed at their unbelief.

Unbelief is based in fear, and you are not in faith when you are in fear. You are not in authority when you are in fear. Fear is often the ultimate enemy in health battles. Why? Because fear is based in death, and we were born into a dying world. Fear constantly says, "You're going to die" when you feel a headache coming on or a hangnail getting infected. Fear takes a mile if you give it just an inch. But friend, fear is a defeated enemy!

The earth curse (Genesis 3) is still in effect, and *fear is the language of the earth curse.* Fear is torment, and it angers me to see it ruining people's lives. So what's the remedy for fear? It's not faith—it's God's love. Perfect love casts out fear! Only God has perfect love, and it's overflowing with security, unconditional acceptance, total abundance, undying devotion, pure motives, faithfulness, joyful affection, self-sacrifice, and beaming pride for you. Wow! Fear is a wimp compared to God's love! *Therefore, to receive healing, we must confront fear with God's love.*

Picture this: Jesus, in all of His eternal glory, is in your house. He is holding out a beautiful box with the biggest diamond ring inside that you've ever seen. With that ring, He is proposing His love to you, saying that if you will make Him your one true love, you can have everything He has (which is a lot)! You can have safety, peace, health, purpose, fulfillment, and more. It won't always be easy to be His bride, because He has plenty of enemies, but He has given you power over those enemies.

One problem: you already have a live-in partner, Fear, who suddenly barges into the room. He demands that you tell Jesus to leave and that you stay with him instead. After all, you are familiar and comfortable with him. He has been with you your whole life. You want to choose Jesus, but you feel helpless to be free of this partner's control. Life with him is not easy, but at least it's predictable; pain, lack, and heartache accompany each day.

Fear says that's all you deserve anyway. He says no one else really loves you and you deserve to suffer. You have played the part of the battered wife or husband for all these years. Why change now?

Just then, Jesus steps between you and Fear. Jesus turns to you and asks, "Do you really want to stay with this jerk?" You look into the eyes of Love, Himself, and He gives you courage. You finally say, "No! I want you, Jesus!" In a flash, Jesus picks up Fear and throws him out into the dark of the night.

You are free! That is, you are free *unless* you choose to open the door of your house once again to that abusive seducer, Fear.

One of my favorite Scriptures is 2 Timothy 1:7 (NLT):

> For God has not given us a spirit of fear and timidity, but of power, love, and self-discipline.

We have a choice between what God has given us and what satan is trying to give us. God has given us power over all the power of satan. He has given us His incredibly strong love. And He has given us the self-discipline to make the right choices with our lives. But it's our choice.

Today I have given you the choice between life and death, between blessings and curses. Now I call on heaven and earth to witness the choice you make. Oh, that you would choose life, so that you and your descendants might live! Deuteronomy 30:19 (NLT).

Are you going to accept Jesus and His gift to you, which includes all the benefits He paid for with His very life? Or are you going to continue living with Fear, allowing him to control your life, listening to his voice?

When the fear in my life was abolished by God's love, it was then that faith and authority could rise. I got bold and confident. I stood a little taller. I stopped having panic attacks. The mental torment ended.

There is so much to be said for making a no-turning-back decision to stand up and act, just like I did that night as I sobbed into the carpet at the beginning of my 30-day healing dare. I got so angry and so tired of putting up with it all that I got daring. I finally stepped into a place of authority. I realized God made me ridiculously in charge of my choices. No one could choose life on my behalf. He was going to honor my choice, my belief, my desires. He was waiting on me.

Authority comes from standing in your God-given position and identity as God's child. Whenever voices of fear try to speak and say, "You're not that strong," you can say, "Maybe not, but my Dad is!" You aren't standing in your own strength. You are walking in the power and strength of Father God. Kicking fear or sickness out of your life is easy when you stand in your rightful place of authority.

Jesus spoke with authority, and the demons obeyed, because He stood in submission to Father God as His commanding officer. He only did what He knew Father God was commissioning Him to do. Therefore, the power of heaven backed up every word He spoke. Likewise, Jesus is our commanding officer, and we can stand with heaven backing up our words of faith.

There was a man in the Bible who truly understood this principle. Matthew 8:8b-10 is the story of a Roman captain who came to Jesus because his servant was dying. Jesus offered to go and heal the servant, but the captain said this:

> "Just say the word, and my servant will be healed. I know this because I am under the authority of my superior officers, and I have authority over my soldiers. I only need to say, 'Go,' and they go, or 'Come,' and they come. And if I say to my slaves, 'Do this,' they do it."

When Jesus heard this, he was

amazed. Turning to those who were following him, he said, "I tell you the truth, I haven't seen faith like this in all Israel!"

This captain knew Jesus's power over the demonic realm, believed in His desire to heal, and understood spiritual authority. *You can have confidence that it is God's desire to heal, and thus, you can stand in a place of authority.* We can know God's will by looking at Jesus. John 5:19 says:

Jesus gave them this answer: "Very truly I tell you, the Son can do nothing by himself; he can do only what he sees his Father doing, because whatever the Father does the Son also does."

Jesus healed ALL who were oppressed of the devil (Acts 10:38). *There was never a time that Jesus sent a person away still sick!* He never said, "I can't heal you because this sickness is my will." He never said, "I'm teaching you a lesson with this leprosy." He never said, "I'm allowing this to happen." No! Jesus healed ALL! Luke 5:12-15 say:

> While Jesus was in one of the towns, a man came along who was covered with leprosy. When he saw Jesus, he fell with his face to the ground and begged him, "Lord, if you are willing, you can make me clean." Jesus reached out his hand and touched the man. "I am willing," he said. "Be clean!" And immediately the leprosy left him.
>
> Then Jesus ordered him, "Don't tell anyone, but go, show yourself to the priest and offer the sacrifices that Moses commanded for your cleansing, as a testimony to them." Yet the news about him spread all the more, so that crowds of people came to hear him and to be healed of their sicknesses.

Jesus proclaimed to this leprous man that it was God's will to heal him, and that has not changed. God doesn't change His mind, and He doesn't show unfair favoritism. What He does for one, He makes available to all through His promises. We receive it as a gift, but we have to take it!

The second way we know God's will and thus walk in our authority is by the leading of the Holy Spirit. He is our Counselor, giving us direction and advice on everything that affects our lives. First Corinthians 2:9-10 say:

> However, as it is written:
> "What no eye has seen, what no ear has heard, and what no human mind has conceived"—the things God has prepared for those who love him—*these are the things God has revealed to us by his Spirit.* The Spirit searches all things, even the deep things of God (emphasis mine).

Then verse 16 goes on to say, **"*But we have the mind of Christ.*"** We are not supposed to walk around without a clue as to what God wants for us. We can know what's on His mind and heart! We are His children, and we have access to His thoughts by the Holy Spirit.

When we know God's will, we can enforce it. We can become crystal clear on God's promises and desires so that we can stand up and speak to the evil that is the source of sickness.

Jesus showed us Father God's nature, and then He gave us His authority. It says in Matthew 10:1:

> Jesus called his twelve disciples to him and gave them authority to drive out impure spirits and to heal every disease and sickness.

The definition of the word *authority* is "the power or right to give orders, make decisions, and enforce obedience." Stand strong! You have been authorized as an agent of change to enforce God's will on Earth as it is in heaven. Your words have power, and the name of Jesus is now given to you. Demonic forces have no choice but to obey words spoken in faith and authority.

Luke 10:19 says:

> I have given you authority to trample on snakes and scorpions and to overcome all the power of the enemy; nothing will harm you.

When we speak words of faith in authority that align with God's will, not only do demons obey, but also angels take actions. *Too many of us have unemployed angels sitting around because we are not speaking words that align with the orders of the Commander-in-Chief.* We are not enforcing the will of God through our declarations.

Angels can only do God's will (bring life more abundantly). They will only enforce words of faith that are spoken in authority. So put those angels to work!

Take action: Speak words of faith with authority, enforcing the victory you already have. Heaven backs you up!

4. PRAY THE PRAYER OF FAITH.

I built my faith for 30 days, but I didn't pray to receive my healing UNTIL I knew faith was there. Why? Because praying is receiving. And to receive, we must be in faith. Going back to the example of receiving a gift, first I have to know that my friend wants to give me the gift, and I must understand that they are trying to hand it to me. When I say, "Thank you" and reach out to take it in my hands, it's mine. The prayer of faith is the reaching out and taking it, saying, "Thank you,

Jesus, that I am healed!"

When I had a clear picture and an unstoppable belief, that was the time to pray. My heart was already celebrating the victory even before I saw it happen! And when we prayed, it was accomplished in the spirit realm, according to Mark 11:24:

> Therefore I tell you, whatever you ask for in prayer, believe that you have received it, and it will be yours.

When do you receive? When you pray, not when it shows up. That's why it's called the prayer of FAITH. You receive what you are praying for when you pray, even if it doesn't instantly appear at that moment. Faith becomes the evidence or the substance of that thing you desire (Hebrews 11:1).

James 5:14-16 say the following about the prayer of faith:

Is anyone among you sick? Let them call the elders of the church to pray over them and anoint them with oil in the name of the Lord. **And the prayer offered in faith will make the sick person well; the Lord will raise them up.** If they have sinned, they will be forgiven. Therefore confess your sins to each other and pray for each other so that you may be healed. The prayer of a righteous person is powerful and effective (emphasis mine).

I had the elders anoint me with oil, come into agreement with my faith, and from that moment, it was finished in my heart. I was healed! I wrote down that date and time.

Let's use the analogy of seed-time and harvest to examine the process of growing our faith. God put seed-time and harvest as a principle that works not only in the physical realm but also in the spiritual realm.

First, the soil of the heart must be prepared. That means any weeds, rocks, or roots need removed. For me, that meant getting rid of some rocks and roots: self-hatred, fear, unforgiveness, and unworthiness. Once those things are removed, it's time to fertilize that soil and fill it with nutrients that will grow seed. We do this through discovering who God is and who we are in Him. That restoration of identity needs to take place. A softening of our hearts happens when we spend time in God's presence worshiping Him and fellowshipping with Him.

Next, we must plant the seeds of the Word of God in our heart (which I did during my 30-day healing dare). The Word of God will produce faith, because faith comes by hearing. A great way to water the harvest is with words of life and thanksgiving. Words of doubt, complaining, ingratitude, gossip, or death are like spraying poison on your crops, so be careful of that!

Finally, it's time to harvest! And faith is the signpost we look for to see that the harvest is ready. We can't pull up the seed before it's time and say, "It didn't work!" It takes patience. When we can see it, we can receive it! When we are walking in confident expectation, it is time to release faith to do its work. My dad calls this "putting the sickle in" with our words of prayer, spoken with authority. Once the harvest is ready, our words harvest it.

Take action: Read Mark 4:26-29 and also check out Your Financial Revolution: The Power of Rest *book by Gary Keesee to learn more about this principle. When your heart is ready to receive, pray the prayer of faith, making your petition to God. You receive when you pray that prayer, so write down the date and time!*

5. PRAISE HIM FOR THE VICTORY.

Even in that time between having the elders pray for me and the morning I woke up healed, which was about two weeks, my faith was still speaking. Despite there being no physical change in the natural, there was a finished work in the supernatural. That's when I just praised God for it, as if it were already finished. I had to keep my eyes fixed on that promise. My faith could see the "after," even when I was still experiencing the "before."

I have seen instantaneous miracles when that prayer of faith happens, but there are also miracles that happen later on after prayer, and recoveries that happen gradually. I have seen all of these scenarios either in my own life or in others' lives, but the ultimate result is the same: healing. Often, there is a process to healing, whether it's the process of building faith, the process of uncovering and receiving deliverance from strongholds, or the process of standing on a promise till a full recovery has happened.

When things don't manifest instantly, we have a choice to make. Will we praise God for what we have already received by faith, or will we slide back into doubt and unbelief? Will we destroy our harvest with words of death, or will we protect and gather our harvest through words of praise and thanksgiving?

Instant deliverance is great, but there's something about standing on a promise by faith that matures you. Your perseverance grows. Your reliance and trust in God grow. *The more resolute in your faith that you become, the more you can receive from God.* That's because you aren't easily moved by circumstances. You don't let go of the Word when satan creates illusions and false evidence meant to convince you of certain doom. He is a master illusionist, but he has no real power until you come into agreement with his illusion!

So when you praise God for the victory even though your physical eyes cannot yet see it, you are turning a blind eye to satan's charades. The less attention you pay to his illusions, the less power they hold. Stop giving his lies any of your attention, and instead, focus back on the Savior.

Hebrews 12:1-3 talk about being resolute in our race, keeping our eyes on the prize like Jesus did:

> Therefore, since we are surrounded by such a great cloud of witnesses, let us throw off everything that hinders and the sin that so easily entangles. And let us run with perseverance the race marked out for us, fixing our eyes on Jesus, the pioneer and perfecter of faith. For the joy set before him he endured

the cross, scorning its shame, and sat down at the right hand of the throne of God. Consider him who endured such opposition from sinners, so that you will not grow weary and lose heart.

Sometimes there's a period of waiting between the "amen" and "there's my healing!" During that time, you are sure to encounter thoughts that don't align with your faith. Don't grow weary! Don't lose heart! Don't allow anything to pull your eyes off of Jesus and what He has already given to you!

The gifts of the Spirit often operate in a corporate setting such as a worship service or large gathering. The gift of healing may flow, and instantaneous healing may take place. That's an awesome thing to behold, and often it is for the purpose of pointing unbelievers to Jesus.

However, unless we know how to

receive and stand on God's promise for ourselves, and take spiritual authority in a situation, we will run from deliverance service to deliverance service with hope but not faith. We will look to a minister to bring that anointing instead of realizing that we have access to that anointing anytime. We will receive prayer from multiple ministers in hope that something happens, only to walk away disappointed. We will beg God for something He has already given to us. Jesus is our Source, not a minister or a revival meeting or a doctor. We have the ability to receive healing anytime, according to our faith.

I believe the process of healing also has to do with being able to hold territory once we take it. For instance, in my life, if I would not have dealt with the roots of the illness—spirits of fear, self-hatred, shame, etc.—I could've opened the door for that illness to come right back. Through the process of freedom and faith building, I became stronger. ***The standing is what makes us stronger!*** In Ephesians 6:13-17, the Apostle Paul equips us for the battle of standing firm:

> Therefore put on the full armor of God, so that when the day of evil comes, you may be able to stand your ground, and ***after you have done everything, to stand. Stand firm then***, with the belt of truth buckled around your waist, with the breastplate of righteousness in place, and with your feet fitted with the readiness that comes from the gospel of peace. In addition to all this, take up the shield of faith, with which you can extinguish all the flaming arrows of the evil one. Take the helmet of salvation and the sword of the Spirit, which is the word of God (emphasis mine).

We must win the battle of our minds if we are to stand on a promise of God.

We must guard our hearts by guarding our thoughts. *What our hearts believe is dictated by the thoughts we think and the words we speak.* Joyce Meyer said:

> No matter how bad the battle rages in your mind, don't give up! Step out and regain the territory that's been stolen from you. Even if it's only an inch at a time, make sure you're leaning on God's grace and not on your own ability. If you don't give up, you'll wear the devil out.

By standing in confident expectation, we keep ourselves in a place to continually receive from Father God. But holding that newly-won territory requires vigilance and a no-negotiating-with-the-enemy attitude.

During those two weeks, I never again asked God to heal me, because that was already done. I didn't beg, plead, cry, or allow discouraging thoughts to take hold.

My confession changed to one of victory and thanksgiving. I acted like I was already healed. I talked like I was already healed. I praised God like I was already healed. I began to say, "Father, thank you that I was healed on Sunday, and I stand on that moment that we prayed according to Mark 11:24. I received it on that day. Now body, you have no choice but to come into alignment with that reality. I thank you, Jesus that you healed me! I'm so grateful."

I want to bring up one more thing that helped me to stand and not doubt, and that was worshiping and fellowshipping with Jesus. My relationship with Him at that point was so much stronger and better than it had been in previous years, because I had spent a lot of time just being with Him.

You see, there were years during which I found myself in a dry season. I had allowed my relationship with Jesus to grow distant. Sure, I knew in my head that God was with me, but I just couldn't seem to feel Him, especially as long as my thoughts were dominated by unworthiness and questioning why this was happening. My love for God had grown cold. I had allowed Him to become less valuable to me than other things in my life. I knew a lot about Him, but I didn't take time to have a relationship with Him.

There's danger in being around religion but not maintaining a relationship with God, Himself. Some of us who have been raised in the church or in "religion" have started slipping away from the love and passion we had for God at first. ***We may want something*** from ***God, but we haven't taken time to first be*** in love ***with Him.*** We have allowed ourselves to become inoculated by the world.

God said in Revelation 2:4 (NLT):

But I have this complaint against you. You don't love me or each other as you did at first!

It's like marriage: once you are around someone long enough, it is easy to stop valuing them. You must consistently invest in the relationship or you won't receive anything out of it. You can't receive from someone if you don't honor them.

You won't receive anything out of a relationship with God if you allow it to become cold, mundane, or based in duty and ritual. That's why praise and worship are so important. They draw our hearts closer to Him.

Worship means "first kiss." If you're a parent, you know how much you love to receive kisses from your child! My little two-year-old puckers his lips and gives me the sweetest kisses before bedtime, and then he smiles and giggles. It's those heart-melting moments that make parenting so joyful. I'm the first woman my little son has loved. I am his "first kiss," and I think that's why there's something so special between a mother and son.

It's the same with my husband and my daughter. They have a very special bond, and it's because he is the first man her little heart has loved. Daddy is her "first kiss." Likewise, Father God is our first kiss. He is the one our hearts were created to love.

In finding a sweet relationship with Him, we truly find ourselves. We find our purpose. ***And Father God just loves to have His kids hanging out in His presence giving Him kisses of thanksgiving. It touches His heart.*** Worship requires taking time to be *with* Him (instead of just hearing *about* Him). And in worship we can experience how truly amazing He is.

Sometimes the best thing you can do when you are in pain is to first put on some great praise music (declarative songs reminding yourself about God's nature and His promises) and proclaim all the things you love about Him. Praise reminds us of who God is and what He can do. ***There is such power in praising***

God because it elevates Him over our problem. We remind ourselves that He is greater than sickness.

Then put on some worship music (that communicates directly to God) and begin to love on Him. Thank Him for who He is. Thank Him for the wonderful love He has given you. It will take your mind off of the problem and get your mind on the answer! And it will help your heart get back in agreement with God—back in faith with His promises to you, even before you see your answer in the natural. When you start speaking words of love to Him, your heart falls back in line.

Investing time in worship is literally investing in God; and when you invest in God, you get the best return in the whole universe—you get Him and everything He has! It is in the presence of the Healer that you will be changed.

When you are in the season of standing, or you are fighting mental battles with thoughts of fear and doubt, I challenge you to get alone and start saying:

> Father, You are so good, and You've been so faithful to me. I praise and honor You for all that you are. I love to be with You because I am your child. I ask You to come and be with me. My soul longs for a glimpse of Your glory. You created the heavens and Earth, and you're so amazing! Nothing is too hard for You! I'm so glad you're my Dad! I praise you! I thank You!

When you start expressing your love for Him through words, dance, and song (you don't have to sound pretty; just be sincere), the King of kings draws closer to you. Your song is His favorite song.

When you worship Him, you give Him permission to come closer to you. I dare you to worship Him until you feel the fear and oppression lift.

You may not know exactly what is going on in your body; maybe you've not been diagnosed yet, or maybe you've received a diagnosis for which doctors have no cure. It doesn't matter, because the Great Physician who made your body knows what is wrong and can lead you to a way of escape. The healing anointing can flow to your body when you worship and spend time in His presence! This is a time to stand and not be shaken. Build a love life with the Healer!

I've gotten to pray with many people who are Christians and yet are angry with God because they've had so many health problems. I pray that my transparency about my past shortcomings and unbelief will open the door for people to confront their own attitudes and ask God to help them believe. I pray that when people hear my story, it uncovers any wrong thinking patterns and moves them from blame to faith.

As long as people blame God, they

can never receive from Him. They have to realize that the real enemy is satan, and he loves to destroy the temples of God—their bodies. But he must leave when they take their rightful authority over him.

I want to tell you a few more amazing stories of people I personally know who have received their healing either through hearing my story or someone else's. Stories help build hope that it can happen for us, and where hope is alive, faith can come in.

Tracy was a spunky, blond gal with a zest for life when she received the crushing diagnosis of debilitating multiple sclerosis. She had numbness all over her body and was told to buy a house that was wheelchair accessible. Doctors have no cure for M.S., and they say that the damage to the brain is irreversible.

But Tracy started coming to Faith Life Church and heard about Jesus, the Healer. She and her husband started commanding the symptoms to leave, and she utterly rejected the diagnosis. Guess what?! The symptoms completely dissipated, and she has been free ever since. That was over 12 years ago. She is now a very active, energetic business owner who is constantly on her feet, moving around, and helping others.

Leah was healed of low self-worth after her husband left her for another woman. Then God healed her of anorexia, which led to healing from multiple sclerosis! He also restored her life, and she is now happily married to a godly man.

Renee was healed of an incurable and rare autoimmune disease that had disabled her and left her with no hope of living. She went from being on her death bed at just 80 pounds to now running her own business and blessing so many with her cheery smile. Today she is healed.

My great-aunt had a cancerous tumor that had been growing swiftly, and doctors scheduled her for surgery. She came to church one weekend and took home the book *Christ the Healer* by F.F. Bosworth, read it that week, and came back for prayer the following Sunday. When we prayed for her, the power of God fell, and she saw a bright light. She said it felt like electricity went through her.

That week when they went to do the operation, they could not find the large baseball-size tumor. It had completely vanished! Doctors were baffled, but she knew why it was gone!

Jennifer had been a lifelong alcoholic. Her addiction had taken over every area of her life, and she was so desperate but had tried AA and everything else she could think of. Finally, she agreed to go to church with her coworker. It was there that she gave her heart to Jesus. That Sunday, after she surrendered to the Savior, she went home to her house and walked right past the refrigerator without stopping for a beer. That's when she realized she didn't even want it. The desire had been taken away! She now helps others who struggle with alcoholism.

Aaron is an Iraq war veteran who came home from the war with severe PTSD, anger issues, insomnia, nightmares, and partial paralysis on his left side from a brain injury. He hadn't slept a full night in years. He couldn't hold on to things because his hand had no strength. His marriage was only intact because his wife refused to give up hope. He was barely coping with day-to-day life and wanted to give up.

At first, he was angry with God over what he was going through, then he heard a teaching about how Jesus healed all. He and his wife really grabbed ahold of God's promises, like the lifeline they so desperately needed.

One weekend, they received prayer and believed for change. That night, he went home and slept for 12 straight hours. He woke up and the paralysis was gone, the nightmares were gone, the PTSD was gone, and he was a brand-new man! He was instantly healed and has spent the years since then sharing with other veterans about the power of Jesus to bring freedom.

Rikki's coworker gave her my book because she had suffered from fibroid tumors for years. They had now grown to the size of baseballs. She was scheduled for a hysterectomy when she picked up my book and began to read. At first, she got angry. She asked God, "Why did you heal Amy but haven't healed me?" And God said, "Because you never asked me."

So she started her own 30-day healing dare, and she asked the Lord to heal her instead of going through surgery. As an act of faith, she even registered for a 5k run to take place the weekend after her scheduled surgery. Every day, she spoke the healing Scriptures at the back of this book, and she focused on the Word. She fasted media and spent time with Jesus. She told me later, "I got serious about this because I wanted it! Surgery isn't a bad thing, but I knew it wasn't a Rikki thing."

One morning, ten days into her 30-day healing dare, she woke up and realized the tumors were completely gone! She, too, had been healed overnight. She called her doctor, but they did not believe her. They refused to see her before her pre-op date. "Ma'am, there's no way on earth those tumors can go away on their own," they told her on the phone.

So she went in for her pre-op visit the day before surgery and demanded that they check and see that the tumors were gone. The nurse went and got the doctor, and when he did the ultrasound, he discovered that the tumors were indeed completely gone! He acted flustered and said, "I'll see you in six months to make sure they haven't come back."

Rikki ran the 5k that weekend with her daughter and celebrated the miracle healing with a girls' weekend that should have been a surgery recovery. But God!

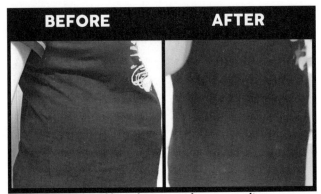

Rikki's fibroid tumors disappeared!

MEETING THE HEALER

God is so amazing, and I will live all my days loving Him. He is my hero! My relationship with Him is the greatest thing I could ever have. The joy of knowing Him has given my life meaning and purpose.

If you don't know what I mean and you just picked up this book because of the crazy before and after picture on the back cover, I want to talk to you for a second.

There really are supernatural forces at work in our world and my story didn't just happen by itself. There is a God who is real, and more than that, who loves YOU!

Until you have had an encounter with THE Creator of all that you see, you will never be truly happy inside. Why? Because God made you, and He is the only One who truly gets you. He understands what makes you tick, what makes you happy, and what you are really capable of. Because God gave you the gift of life, He also has the perfect plan for your life. He is just waiting with open arms to heal you, not only physically but also emotionally and mentally, as well. His power is crazy awesome, and you will never find a love like His anywhere else in this world.

Romans 3:23-25a says:

> For all have sinned and fall short of the glory of God, and all are justified freely by his grace through the redemption that came by Christ Jesus. God presented Christ as a sacrifice of atonement, through the shedding of his blood—to be received by faith.

None of us are holy or perfect, so God gave His Son Jesus as a sacrifice to pay for our wrongs. Jesus said, "Let me take their punishment instead, so they can take my holiness."

Although Jesus died a horrible death

on a Roman-made cross (an instrument of torture and death), He was ultimately too powerful for death. He rose up from the gave and came back to life. Then He gave that same power over death to anyone who will believe in Him. He ended the fear of death once and for all!

If you want to receive that forgiveness and freedom, if you want to meet God and start living a life full of His power, just talk to Him wherever you are right now, because He is right there with you. Simply ask Him to come into your life, forgive you of your sins, and to be your God (John 3:16, Romans 10:9).

You can say something like:

"God, I believe you are real and that Jesus came to take my punishment so I could be holy. I believe that You love me and want to have a relationship with me. Forgive me for trying to live without You. Touch me right now with Your power. I give You my life and ask You to make something good out of it. Amen."

If you just prayed that prayer, right now angels are throwing a party for you in heaven! Heaven is now your home because you have accepted God as your Father. You do not have to fear anything because, "the one who is in you is greater than the one who is in the world" (1 John 4:4).

In other words, God inside of you is greater than the evil that is in this world!

I encourage you to read the Bible (start with the books of Mark and Romans), find a church that is alive and teaches God's Word, and get to know others who are Christ's followers. Your life has just taken a turn for the best!

CHAPTER FOUR

COMMON MISCONCEPTIONS ABOUT HEALING

"But woe to you, scribes and Pharisees, hypocrites, because you shut off the kingdom of heaven from people; for you do not enter in yourselves, nor do you allow those who are entering to go in."
Matthew 23:13 (NASB)

I would like to answer a few more of the most common objections and questions about supernatural healing. When I claim that Jesus wants to heal everyone, it can offend some people. After all, it seems radical to this fallen world's state of sickness and death.

Every time you try to believe God for something like healing, satan is immediately going to try and convince you otherwise. He doesn't want you healed or prosperous or changing other people's lives! He wants you broke, sick, fearful, angry, and depressed. That's where we have a choice: who are we going to listen to? Are we going to listen to satan or to those he uses to tout his message of fear and death? Or are we going to run to God's message and listen to what He has to say?

If you've been taught a lot about how God brings or allows suffering, let me challenge you to open your mind to what the Word says. Some things are traditions of men based on human experience and not on Truth. Healing is one of God's promises, but it's up to you to believe it.

"DID GOD REALLY SAY...?"

I have addressed this question throughout this book, but satan will always whisper, "Did God really say He would heal you?" That's exactly what he said to Eve when he deceived her into disobeying God. His first line of defense is to plant seeds of doubt and subvert the Truth. He doesn't have any new tricks up his sleeve, just the same old same old.

One day I heard my child talking to their sibling and trying to convince them it was okay to disobey what I had instructed. "She didn't really MEAN we couldn't do it at all," said the child. And I thought, *Wow, that's the sin nature we were all born with.* Needless to say, I stepped in and made my will very clearly known to that child. Haha! The flesh tries to get its way, while disregarding, blaming, or disobeying God.

That's why it's so crucial to KNOW the Word. Scripture memorization isn't just for kids in Sunday school! It's the lifeline to a life worth living.

We can also fill our minds with so many intellectual arguments, theological reasonings, and denominational traditions that we simply cannot become like a child and just receive from God. That simple trust can be lost when we allow our minds to take over the leadership of our lives. Here's what Paul, who was trained as a Pharisee, said about human reasoning in relation to the Gospel:

> Dear brothers and sisters, I want you to understand that the gospel message I preach is not based on mere human reasoning.
>
> —Galations 1:11 (NLT)

We use God's mighty weapons, not worldly weapons, to knock down the strongholds of human reasoning and to destroy false arguments.

—2 Corinthians 10:4 (NLT)

And it is impossible to please God without faith. Anyone who wants to come to him must believe that God exists and that he rewards those who sincerely seek him.

—Hebrews 11:6 (NLT)

The message of the cross is foolish to those who are headed for destruction! But we who are being saved know it is the very power of God.

—1 Corinthians 1:18 (NLT)

Paul knew that satan tries to argue against God using our human reasoning. If we are living out of only what our minds can understand, we will never see the power of

God manifest. We will constantly question, "Did God really say...?"

Many preachers have even taught the assumption that we must live in the dark, never really knowing for sure any of God's will. I have already dealt with this argument, but I want to encourage you that as a child of God you can indeed know what God said, through His Word, through the Holy Spirit, through words of prophecy that confirm the Word, and through wise instruction by Bible believing pastors.

The supernatural looks impossible to the natural mind, so when objections arise in our thought lives we must cast them down. Faced with many doubts, Abraham stood on the promise of God, even though it looked ridiculously impossible:

> Yet he [Abraham] did not waver through unbelief regarding the promise of God, but was strengthened in his faith and gave glory to God, being fully

persuaded that God had power to do what he had promised.

—Romans 4:20-21

"GOD IS TEACHING YOU THROUGH SUFFERING."

People have used the following Scripture to argue that God uses bad things to bring good in our lives.

> And we know that in all things God works for the good of those who love him, who have been called according to his purpose.
>
> —Romans 8:28

It says, "IN all things," not "when God causes all things." God doesn't cause everything. He is not the originator of all the circumstances we will face. We live in a fallen world inhabited by evil. Yet, He is such a good Father that He will bring good out of bad situations if we will trust Him. He will bring healing where there has been sickness. He will bring purpose out of pain. He will turn around those ashes and make something beautiful. Nothing is beyond His redemptive power!

You've probably heard the saying, "God will make a message out of your mess, and He will make a testimony out of your test." The bad was not required to get to the good, but He will still turn it around and redeem it!

People get offended and say, "Amy, how dare you insinuate that I missed it or that it was my fault something bad happened," but in their next breath they insinuate that it was God's fault. ***They would rather place the blame on God instead of accepting personal responsibility or exposing that it is the devil who is to blame.*** My God is not a child abuser. We might step outside of His loving protection, but He never abandons us.

I'm not saying people deserve all the bad things that happen to them. And I'm also not condemning anyone who has made mistakes. I lived in a wrong mind set for many years. That's on me, not God. He is still merciful. He is angry with what the devil has tried to do against us. I certainly don't want anyone to feel condemned. Just put the blame in the wrong place.

Ultimately, the devil is the one to blame. And even though we might lose some battles in weak moments, that's okay. We have already won the war, so there's no such thing as defeat for a Christian unless they quit on God. Heaven is our home! We have the Kingdom! No matter what we face in this life, it's not our final destination.

Here's another thought. If God uses sickness to teach us, why did Jesus heal all? Why didn't he ever say, "Oh no, that leprosy is teaching you patience." Not ONE TIME did Jesus tell someone that the sickness was from Him.

Like Pastor Bill Johnson says, "You cannot give what you don't have. God isn't sick, nor was Jesus sick."

Another Scripture people use to argue that sometimes, God causes infirmity is from John 9:1-5 (NKJV):

> Now as Jesus passed by, He saw a man who was blind from birth. And His disciples asked Him, saying, "Rabbi, who sinned, this man or his parents, that he was born blind?"
>
> Jesus answered, "Neither this man nor his parents sinned, but that the works of God should be revealed in him. I must work the works of Him who sent Me while it is day; the night is coming when no one can work. As long as I am in the world, I am the light of the world."

Let me ask you this: who added the punctuation to this sentence? It was the translators, because there were no commas or periods in ancient Aramaic. When it was translated, punctuation was added. Now, what happens when I change just a few punctuation marks in verse 3? It would read:

> Jesus answered, "Neither this man nor his parents sinned. But that the works of God should be revealed in him, I must work the works of Him who sent Me while it is day."

The meaning changes. There are other translations that add "*nevertheless,* that the works of God should be revealed...."

Others have commented that the intended meaning before translation is more in line with the thought that from birth, God chose the blind man to be evidence that Jesus was the Messiah. He was destined to display the glory of God, not that God decided before he was born to inflict him with blindness. He had a date with destiny on that day when Jesus noticed him.

Whichever one of these theories fits, and all seem plausible, we must read with the filter of God's goodness. I don't pretend to be a scholar, but I do know that when we look at Scripture through the lens of God's character being good, we stop seeing God as the cause of suffering, and instead, see Him as the cure. Jesus's ministry was marked by healing, freedom, and most of all, love:

> News about him spread all over Syria, and people brought to him all who were ill with various diseases, those suffering severe pain, the demon-possessed, those having seizures, and the paralyzed; and he healed them.
>
> —Matthew 4:24

> Jesus rebuked the demon, and it came out of the boy, and he was healed at that moment.
>
> —Matthew 17:18

A large crowd followed him, and he healed all who were ill.

—Matthew 12:15

Great crowds came to him, bringing the lame, the blind, the crippled, the mute and many others, and laid them at his feet; and he healed them.

—Matthew 15:30

By faith in the name of Jesus, this man whom you see and know was made strong. It is Jesus' name and the faith that comes through him that has completely healed him, as you can all see.

—Acts 3:16

"GOD ALLOWS SICKNESS SOMETIMES."

Not only does God not give us sickness, but He also is not the one who allows it in our lives. WE are the only ones who, however the sickness originated, allow it to stay by not taking our rightful authority. Sickness is present because we don't fully understand our healing covenant. WE HAVE BEEN GIVEN THE COVENANT AUTHORITY BY GOD to trample on illnesses and be raised up out of them. Please read Matthew 16:9, Luke 9:1, Luke 10:19, and James 5:14-18.

What God does for one, He will do for all who have faith. Peter said, "...I now realize how true it is that God does not show favoritism" (Acts 10:34). He is just and fair. But He has given the authority to us on Earth to make our own decisions, form our own allegiances, and receive whatever we choose to believe.

ISN'T GOD SOVEREIGN?

Yes, He is sovereign, but in His sovereignty, He already made the choice to heal all. So no, He cannot do whatever He wants because He will not violate His Word or His promises or His character. He will not withhold that which He has already decided to give, according to His covenant.

Jesus read Isaiah 61:1 on the first day of His public ministry. The very first line calls the Lord "sovereign," and then it goes on to tell us what God in His sovereignty chose to do through Jesus.

> The Spirit of the Sovereign Lord is on me, because the Lord has anointed me to proclaim good news to the poor. He has sent me to bind up the brokenhearted, to proclaim freedom for the captives and release from darkness for the prisoners....

I also love Psalm 84:11-12 (AMP):

> For the Lord God is a sun and shield; The Lord bestows grace and

favor and honor; ***No good thing will He withhold from those who walk uprightly.*** O Lord of hosts, how blessed and greatly favored is the man who trusts in You [believing in You, relying on You, and committing himself to You with confident hope and expectation] (Emphasis mine).

And Hebrews 6:17 (NLT) is amazing, showing us that God doesn't make erratic decisions or change His mind. It says:

God also bound himself with an oath, so that those who received the promise could be perfectly sure that he would never change his mind.

"WHAT ABOUT JOB'S TROUBLES?"

Okay, here we go. It's probably the most asked about story in the Bible when we talk about healing. It's also the most misquoted and misunderstood. I do not have time to get deep into this one, but I will give several points, and I encourage you to listen to the series "Why? Big Questions for God" by Gary Keesee for further insight.

Okay, here are several thoughts on the story of Job:

First of all, Job was a man without a covenant. He was alive before Abraham, and Job is actually one of the oldest books in the Bible. Job did not have the Abrahamic Covenant or the New Covenant that we have today. Therefore, satan had a legal right to mess with him. That's what the conversation we read about between God and satan is all about in the beginning. Satan is basically saying, "Hey, hold on one moment. This guy isn't above the earth curse. He has no covenant!" God agrees that satan has a legal right to tempt Job.

Job has fear in his life. He is constantly making sacrifices to God on behalf of the sins of his children. He says in Job 3:25 (NLT), "What I always feared has happened to me. What I dreaded has come true." Fear is a magnet that attracts the very thing you fear. It draws those things to you because it is faith in reverse. It is a belief that something is going to happen, even though that something is bad.

Third, Job had a wrong perception of God. We hear what Job really believed when the pressure was applied to his life, and it's not pretty. Here are Job 9:16-17, 21-24b (NLT):

> And even if I summoned him and he responded, I'm not sure he would listen to me. For he attacks me with a storm and repeatedly wounds me without cause. I am innocent, but it makes no difference to me—I despise my life. Innocent or wicked, it is all the same to God. That's why I say, "He destroys both the blameless and

the wicked." When a plague sweeps through, he laughs at the death of the innocent. If he's not the one who does it, who is?

Whoa. God sounds like a terrible person in this passage! Job's friends rebuke him, saying:

> You have said, "My doctrine is sound, and I am pure in Your sight." But if only God would speak and open His lips against you, and disclose to you the secrets of wisdom, for true wisdom has two sides.
>
> —Job 11:4-5

Job goes on and on in chapter after chapter about how God is wronging him and how he is a righteous man, never having done anything wrong. Three friends try to reason with him and show him the error of his thinking, albeit in a condemning fashion. But Job will hear none of it. Job 32:1-2 (NLT) says:

> So these three men stopped answering Job, because he was righteous in his own eyes. But Elihu son of Barakel the Buzite, of the family of Ram, became very angry with Job for ***justifying himself rather than God*** (emphasis mine).

Finally, the youngest of Job's friends cannot take anymore. He speaks up, seeing that Job has a serious pride issue, while having no problem casting blame on God. Elihu comes to God's defense and says:

> Listen to me, you who have understanding. Everyone knows that God doesn't sin. The Almighty can do no wrong. He repays people according to their deeds. He treats people as they deserve. Truly, God will not do wrong.

> The Almighty will not twist justice.
> —Job 34:10-12 (NLT)

Then, it's God's turn to speak to Job, and we see God rebukes his attitude and wrong perceptions for ***three whole chapters***.

> Then the Lord answered Job from the whirlwind: "Who is this that questions my wisdom with such ignorant words?
> —Job 38:1-2 (NLT)

> Will you discredit my justice and condemn me just to prove you are right?
> —Job 40:8 (NLT)

Bam. There's the heart of the matter. ***Job is justifying himself but in the process is blaming and condemning God.*** And I get it. People who are in pain sometimes curse the very one who can help them.

Job is quick to repent. He says:

I had only heard about you before, but now I have seen you with my own eyes. I take back everything I said, and I sit in dust and ashes to show my repentance.

—Job 42:5-6 (NLT)

God then blesses Job with double what he had before, and he became one of the richest men in the world. He lived 140 years more and saw his fourth generation. All in all, scholars estimate that Job's troubles lasted for a couple of months and certainly no longer than a year. But the blessing that followed his repentance lasted for four generations!

The point is, don't use Job's troubles as an excuse to blame God or to excuse years of putting up with calamity. Don't accuse God of being unjust so that you can justify yourself. Ouch. I know. It's a tough lesson to learn, but it's one I, too, had to settle in my heart.

"HEALING PASSED AWAY."

The doctrine of "cessationism," the belief that miracles died with the apostles, is one of the most baffling things to me. With so many documented inexplicable supernatural healings that have happened around the world since then, you would think this false doctrine would also have died out by now.

With this logic, we might as well say that everything else Jesus taught about and demonstrated also passed away with the disciples. *Either everything Jesus did and said will endure forever, or none of it will.* God Himself said, "I the Lord do not change…" (Malachi 3:6a). Here are more scriptures on this subject:

> Heaven and earth will pass away, but my words will never pass away.
> —Matthew 24:35

God is not human, that he should lie, not a human being, that he should change his mind. Does he speak and then not act? Does he promise and not fulfill?

—Numbers 23:19

Every good and perfect gift is from above, coming down from the Father of the heavenly lights, who does not change like shifting shadows.

—James 1:17

If we still believe what Jesus said, we can still do what He did:

Very truly I tell you, whoever believes in me will do the works I have been doing, and they will do even greater things than these, because I am going to the Father.

—John 14:12

My prayer is not for them [the disciples] alone. I pray also for those who will believe in me through their message, that all of them may be one, Father, just as you are in me and I am in you. May they also be in us so that the world may believe that you have sent me. I have given them the glory that you gave me, that they may be one as we are one.

—John 17:20-22

Whoever believes can do the same works as Jesus did and even greater works because now we have the Holy Spirit dwelling in us! No, miracles have not passed away! We're just getting started! Jesus has prayed for us. He looked into the future of mankind and saw us! He gave us His glory, and if we remain in Him, we can flow in His life-giving power to cast out demons, heal the sick, and see lives changed forever.

The amazing works of the apostles are a

taste of what we, as believers, are capable of doing through Christ Jesus.

> As a result, people brought the sick into the streets and laid them on beds and mats so that at least Peter's shadow might fall on some of them as he passed by. Crowds gathered also from the towns around Jerusalem, bringing their sick and those tormented by impure spirits, and *__all of them__* were healed (emphasis mine).
>
> —Acts 5:15

Satan is the father of all lies, and of course, his number one job is to lie about God, about our covenant, and about us. The question is, will you believe him or will you believe what God says?

"WHAT ABOUT PAUL'S THORN IN THE FLESH?"

In the book of Corinthians, and especially in the chapters surrounding the famous "thorn in the flesh" passage, Paul is being very honest with a church that is following after ungodly doctrines, living in sin, speaking gossip, and even murmuring against him. Paul is laying out the case for why they should listen to him, and he talks about how much he has suffered for the sake of the Gospel. In 2 Corinthians 11:23b-26, which is right before the passage about the thorn, he describes the intense persecution he has undergone:

> I have worked much harder, been in prison more frequently, been flogged more severely, and been exposed to death again and again. Five times I received from the Jews the forty lashes minus one. Three times

I was beaten with rods, once I was pelted with stones, three times I was shipwrecked, I spent a night and a day in the open sea, I have been constantly on the move. I have been in danger from rivers, in danger from bandits, in danger from my fellow Jews, in danger from Gentiles; in danger in the city, in danger in the country, in danger at sea; and in danger from false believers.

And then the famous passage, which has been the subject of so much false doctrine concerning sickness:

Therefore, in order to keep me from becoming conceited, I was given a thorn in my flesh, a messenger of Satan, to torment me. Three times I pleaded with the Lord to take it away from me. But he said to me, "My grace is sufficient for you, for my power is made perfect in weakness." Therefore I will boast all the more gladly about my weaknesses, so that Christ's power may rest on me. That is why, for Christ's sake, I delight in weaknesses, In insults, in hardships, in persecutions, in difficulties. For when I am weak, then I am strong.

—2 Corinthians 12:7b-10

So what was the thorn in the flesh? We don't have to guess, because Paul tells us it was a messenger of satan, a demon, sent on assignment to stir up persecution against him. It would incite violence among the people, the local governments, and even within the church folk. The demon stirred up insults, hardships, persecutions, and difficulties caused by people who were under the influence of that demon, and thus caused Paul pain.

Paul is actually using a common Jewish metaphor of the time. There are several other passages that refer to "thorns" as difficult people (not infirmities). Numbers 33:55 says:

> But if you do not drive out the inhabitants of the land, those you allow to remain will become barbs in your eyes and thorns in your sides. They will give you trouble in the land where you will live.

See also Joshua 23:13 and Judges 2:3, both of which use the phrase "thorn" in reference to evil people who will bring persecution against God's people. (It reminds me of the fact that Jesus took a spear to his side when He paid the price for our ultimate freedom!)

Paul was having people trouble, and that's the worst kind of trouble. It resulted in beatings, constant danger, and incredible pressure to stop preaching, but he didn't quit.

His body bore scars from the many things he went through, but he was always raised up each time. He was even able to walk miles and miles to the next town after just being stoned and left for dead! The power of God kept his body going until he had completed his race.

Paul signed up for the persecution because he knew it was worth it. He stepped into the arena. He gladly gave his life for the sake of the Gospel. Matthew 16:24-25 (ESV) says:

> Then Jesus told his disciples, "If anyone would come after me, let him deny himself and take up his cross and follow me. For whoever would save his life will lose it, but whoever loses his life for my sake will find it."

Guess what? We have not been redeemed from persecution. In fact, Jesus promised we would have it if we follow Him and live boldly. It shouldn't surprise us when we are persecuted by people for our faith. There will be those who hate the Truth and hate the message. I myself have encountered persecution, hate mail, and have lost friends because of my beliefs. That's okay! We should count it an honor to take up our crosses and follow Christ. ***Suffering from persecution is something that comes with the territory. Suffering from a spirit of infirmity is something we have been given authority over.***

Andrew Wommack says, "Satan has used traditional teaching about Paul's thorn to bring many Christians to a place of submitting to him."

Instead, let's submit to God, resist the devil, and he must flee (James 4:7). After all, the safest place we can be is in the will of God.

> "Thus you nullify the word of God by your tradition that you have handed down."
>
> —Mark 7:13

CHAPTER FIVE

TOOLS
FOR A WINNING
BATTLE

"For though we live in the world, we do not wage war as the world does. The weapons we fight with are not the weapons of the world. On the contrary, they have divine power to demolish strongholds. We demolish arguments and every pretension that sets itself up against the knowledge of God, and we take captive every thought to make it obedient to Christ."

2 Corinthians 10:3-5

No one can ever convince me that God isn't real, because I've seen His work with my own eyes. And no one can ever tell me that He doesn't heal, because He healed me. Let's recap the steps God took me through to receive my miracle.

If you need healing in your body:

1. Reclaim your identity. Let the Holy Spirit minister value and worth to your soul. As you read the Bible, ask the Holy Spirit to show you who you are in Him. Spend time saying, "Father, I belong to You. I'm your beloved child in whom You are well pleased. I am perfectly safe and secure in Your love. Healed is who I am. Joyful is who I am. Loved is who I am."

2. Repaint your picture, using the 30-day healing dare to build your faith. I dare you to saturate your life with God's Truth to you about healing, both emotionally and physically. Speak it out loud multiple times a day, and shut off all the other distractions. Ask God to show you if there is unforgiveness, bitterness, or anger in your heart. Confess it, and then go to the person you have those feelings toward to make it right. Let go of all malice, bitterness, envy, gossip, or other soul-realm maladies.

3. *Stand in your authority.* Take up your rightful place of authority as a child of God, and stand in that place of agreement with His Word. Chase away any fearful thoughts with words of faith, and know that fear has no place in your life! Read through Romans 8:14-17:

> For those who are led by the Spirit of God are the children of God. The Spirit you received does not make you slaves, so that you live in fear again; rather, the Spirit you received brought about your adoption to sonship. And by him we cry, "Abba, Father." The Spirit himself testifies with our spirit that we are God's children. Now if we are children, then we are heirs—heirs of

God and co-heirs with Christ, if indeed we share in his sufferings in order that we may also share in his glory.

4. *Pray the prayer of faith when you are totally convinced.* When you come to a place where you have joy in your heart instead of fear, and you know without a doubt it is God's will to heal you, it's time to pray! Pray with the elders of your church or someone who you know believes in healing. It is very important who you have pray with you because you are partnering with their faith. Make sure they agree with what God said about healing.

5. *Praise Him for the victory!*

Once you pray that prayer of agreement, write down that date and time and hold on to that moment as the moment you were healed. Mark the spot and stand on it! Ignore what you feel like—simply believe! It is finished, and your faith is all the evidence you need that you are already healed. Your healing may show up physically in that moment, or it may be a process. Sometimes there is a recovery period instead of an instant manifestation. But stay in agreement with God for a full recovery! "...they shall lay hands on the sick, and they shall recover" (Mark 16:18b, KJV).

Stand strong and continue sowing the Word in your heart. Faith comes by ***hearing*** the Word. Notice that word "hearing" is an active, present tense verb, meaning we have to keep hearing and hearing to be able to stay in faith. It can't just be what we heard. It has to be what we are hearing! Why? Because we live in a world of fear, and every day we are hearing news of death and destruction. If we don't continually inundate our minds with the power of God's words, we will begin to listen and believe all the voices of fear.

I'm telling you, no matter how impossibly difficult your sickness seems, no matter what doctors or relatives have told you, there is a Greater One on the inside of you, and He is just waiting to release His healing anointing in your life! I'm so excited just thinking about what is going to happen in your body as you drench your life with God's Word on healing!

HEALING CONFESSIONS

This is a confession I want you to pray over yourself daily as you believe for total health:

"Father, thank You that You love me, and You call me precious. I submit myself to You right now. You are my King and Sovereign. I ask You to clean my heart of any sin or unrighteousness. I forgive and release anyone who has harmed me. I forgive myself, and I bind condemnation. I belong to You. My best days are ahead of me!

"I praise You for Your promises to me! You said that the same resurrection power that brought Jesus out of the grave is now restoring and quickening my mortal body. I receive it now. I believe that You sent Jesus to pay the price for my healing. You said that by His wounds, I am healed. I believe Your Word is true for me today.

"I command the spirit of infirmity to leave my body now and never return! You evil spirit of sickness, I belong to God Most High, and according to the blood Jesus shed on the Cross, I have authority over you. I bind you and command you to go! Every symptom must leave! Pain, be gone, in Jesus's name. I will live and not die and will declare the works of the Lord. Greater is He that is in me than anything in this world. I've been given power to trample on the enemy, and nothing shall by any means harm me.

"Body, I call forth the anointing on the inside of me to flood you with life. I command you to line up with God's Truth. You are healed! God said it, and I believe it. It is finished! Amen."

Now, spend time speaking to specific body parts to be normal. Command illness, disease, tumors, or anything else violating your body to wither and die at the roots. The power of life and death is in your words.

Now, I want to challenge you to meditate on the Word of God constantly, as if it is your very breath. Speak it out loud. Think about it all day. Let it roll around in your mind and spirit.

The Word of God is made of spirit, just like your body is made of cells. When you speak the healing Word, you are literally rebuilding your body in the spirit realm cell by cell. Soon it will be visible in the natural realm!

Here are some scriptures to get you started!

HEALING SCRIPTURES TO STAND ON:

Surely he took up our pain and bore our suffering, yet we considered him punished by God, stricken by him, and afflicted. But he was pierced for our transgressions, he was crushed for our iniquities; the punishment that brought us peace was on him, and by his wounds we are healed.

—Isaiah 53:4-5

But if the Spirit of him that raised up Jesus from the dead dwell in you, he that raised up Christ from the dead shall also quicken your mortal bodies by his Spirit that dwelleth in you.

—Romans 8:11 (KJV)

"...they shall lay hands on the sick, and they shall recover."

—Mark 16:18b (KJV)

I have given you authority to trample on snakes and scorpions and to overcome all the power of the enemy; nothing will harm you.

—Luke 10:19

Praise the Lord, my soul, and forget not all his benefits—who forgives all your sins and heals all your diseases.

—Psalm 103:2-3

Dear friend, I pray that you may enjoy good health and that all may go well with you, even as your soul is getting along well.

—3 John 1:2

He will take our weak mortal bodies and change them into glorious bodies like his own, using the same power with which he will bring everything under his control.

—Philippians 3:21 (NLT)

TOOLS FOR A WINNING BATTLE

Is anyone among you sick? Then he must call for the elders of the church and they are to pray over him, anointing him with oil in the name of the Lord; and the prayer offered in faith will restore the one who is sick, and the Lord will raise him up, and if he has committed sins, they will be forgiven him.

—James 5:14-15

"Yet he did not waver through unbelief regarding the promise of God, but was strengthened in his faith and gave glory to God, being fully persuaded that God had power to do what he had promised."

—Romans 4:20-21 (talking about Abraham)

He sent his word and healed them; he rescued them from the grave.

—Psalm 107:20

When Jesus came into Peter's house, he saw Peter's mother-in-law lying in bed with a fever. He touched her hand and the fever left her, and she got up and began to wait on him. When evening came, many who were demon-possessed were brought to him, and he drove out the spirits with a word and healed all the sick. This was to fulfill what was spoken through the prophet Isaiah: "He took up our infirmities and carried our diseases."

—Matthew 8:14-17

They will have no fear of bad news; their hearts are steadfast, trusting in the Lord.

—Psalm 112:7

Lord my God, I called to you for help and you healed me.

—Psalm 30:2

Jesus turned and saw her. "Take heart, daughter," he said, "your faith has healed you." And the woman was healed from that moment.

—Matthew 9:22

Heal me, Lord, and I will be healed; save me and I will be saved, for you are the one I praise.

—Jeremiah 17:14

And you know that God anointed Jesus of Nazareth with the Holy Spirit and with power. Then Jesus went around doing good and healing all who were oppressed by the devil, for God was with him.

—Acts 10:38, (NLT)

Let God be true, and every human being a liar.

—Romans 3:4

Now faith is the substance of things hoped for, the evidence of things not seen.

—Hebrews 11:1 (KJV)

For no matter how many promises God has made, they are "Yes" in Christ. And so through him the "Amen" is spoken by us to the glory of God.

—2 Corinthians 1:20

The thief comes only to steal and kill and destroy; I have come that they may have life, and have it to the full.

—John 10:10

Or do you not know that your body is a temple of the Holy Spirit who is in you, whom you have from God, and that you are not your own? For you have been bought with a price: therefore glorify God in your body.

—1 Corinthians 6:19-20

Therefore I say unto you, What things soever ye desire, when ye pray, believe that ye receive them, and ye shall have them.

—Mark 11:24 (KJV)

But for you who fear my name, the Sun of Righteousness will rise with healing in his wings. And you will go free, leaping with joy like calves let out to pasture.

—Malachi 4:2 (NLT)

It has come at last—salvation and power and the Kingdom of our God, and the authority of his Christ. For the accuser of our brothers and sisters has been thrown down to earth—the one who accuses them before our God day and night. And they have defeated him by the blood of the Lamb and by their testimony.

—Revelation 12:10-12a (NLT)

So they set out and went from village to village, proclaiming the good news and healing people everywhere.

—Luke 9:6

...who had come to hear him and to be healed of their diseases. Those troubled by impure spirits were cured, and the people all tried to touch him, because power was coming from him and healing them all.

—Luke 6:18-19

God also bound himself with an oath, so that those who received the promise could be perfectly sure that he would never change his mind.

—Hebrews 11:6 (NLT)

I will exalt you, Lord, for you rescued me. You refused to let my enemies triumph over me. Lord my God, I cried to you for help, and you restored my health. You brought me up from the grave, O Lord. You kept me from falling into the pit of death. Weeping may last through the night, but joy comes with the morning. You have turned my mourning into joyful dancing.

—Psalm 30:1-3, 5, and 11-12 (NLT)

You will not fear the terror of night, nor the arrow that flies by day, nor the pestilence that stalks in the darkness, nor the plague that destroys at midday. A thousand may fall at your side, ten thousand at your right hand, but it will not come near you.

—Psalm 91:5-7

Nevertheless, I will bring health and healing to it; I will heal my people and will let them enjoy abundant peace and security.

—Jeremiah 33:6

ABOUT
Amy Keesee Freudiger

As an author, speaker, worship leader, and singer/songwriter, Amy Keesee Freudiger has a passion to see people encounter the presence of the Living God, just as she did when she was miraculously and instantly healed of a thirteen pound tumor.

Since then, Amy has been on a mission to set others free from infirmity. Her compassion, bold faith, and sensitivity to God's presence have resulted in many others being healed.

Amy has always had a heart to see generational revival and supernatural healing in families. She is the Worship Pastor at Faith Life Church in New Albany, Ohio, and is a singer/songwriter with their worship band Open Heaven (www.openheaven.com).

Amy lives near Columbus, Ohio with her husband, Jason, and their daughter Journey and sons Dawson and Revere.

Check out my blog!
www.healedovernight.com

Connect with me on social media!
www.facebook.com/amyfreudiger
Instagram: @amyfreudiger
Twitter: @amyfreudiger

Write me:
Faith Life Church
Attn: Amy Freudiger
2407 Beech Rd.
New Albany, OH 43054